Praise for *Let's Look*

"*Let's Look Together* is a gem in the realm ᴏ... ...
—immersing us in Nouwen's transparent way through his life and writings as well as in the author's own engagement and furthering of Nouwen's insights. It's also an invitation into self-mentoring as we ourselves partake, appropriate, and personalize both their combined offerings to us all. Truly a welcome gift to receive!"

—Wil Hernandez, PhD, Obl., OSB
spiritual director, author, *Mere Spirituality:
The Spiritual Life According to Henri Nouwen*

"Dr. Robert Wicks in *Let's Look Together* provides an insightful, accessible, and timeless approach to Henri Nouwen as a spiritual mentor. Dr. Wicks' prodigious mind draws from the worlds of scripture, theology, philosophy, and psychiatry and weaves them into a rich tapestry of story and prayerful understanding. The reader understands Nouwen better and themselves better. Dr. Wicks has given us a gift in this precious work—a gem of a book!"

—Julianne Stanz, author, *Braving the Thin Places*

"There is nothing better than learning from two great spiritual mentors at once. Robert Wicks guides the reader through some of the essential wisdom of Henri Nouwen with depth and clarity. The four key themes of Henri's spiritual insight—desert wilderness, ordinariness, compassion and community, and vulnerability and prayer—offer both novices and seasoned spiritual practitioners a new way to think, reflect, feel, and see on the journey of faith and discovery. Wicks has given us all a gift by sharing his experience of Nouwen as a personal spiritual mentor and by inviting us to be accompanied by Nouwen's spiritual wisdom along our own journeys."

—Daniel P. Horan, OFM, Saint Mary's College
author, *The Way of the Franciscans*

Also by Robert J. Wicks

Let's Look Together

Let's Look Together

Henri Nouwen as Spiritual Mentor

Robert J. Wicks
author of *Riding the Dragon*

ORBIS BOOKS

Maryknoll, New York 10545

Founded in 1970, Orbis Books endeavors to publish works that enlighten the mind, nourish the spirit, and challenge the conscience. The publishing arm of the Maryknoll Fathers and Brothers, Orbis seeks to explore the global dimensions of the Christian faith and mission, to invite dialogue with diverse cultures and religious traditions, and to serve the cause of reconciliation and peace. The books published reflect the views of their authors and do not represent the official position of the Maryknoll Society. To learn more about Maryknoll and Orbis Books, please visit our website at www.orbisbooks.com.

Manufactured in the United States of America

Library of Congress Cataloging-in-Publication Data

Names: Wicks, Robert J., author.
Title: Let's look together : Henri Nouwen as spiritual mentor / Robert
    J. Wicks, author of Riding the dragon.
Other titles: Let us look together
Description: Maryknoll, New York : Orbis Books, [2023] | Includes
    bibliographical references.
Identifiers: LCCN 2022044990 (print) | LCCN 2022044991 (ebook) | ISBN
    9781626985223 (print) | ISBN 9781608339617 (ebook)
Subjects: LCSH: Nouwen, Henri J. M.—Ethics. | Catholic
    Church—Clergy—Netherlands—Religious life. | Catholic
    Church—Clergy—United States—Religious life. | Spiritual direction. |
    Mentoring—Religious aspects—Christianity. | Spiritual life—Catholic Church
Classification: LCC BX1912.5 .W53 2023 (print) | LCC BX1912.5 (ebook) |
    DDC 232/.8—dc23/eng/20221130
LC record available at https://lccn.loc.gov/2022044990
LC ebook record available at https://lccn.loc.gov/2022044991

For the Carmelite Sisters of Baltimore

Contents

III
SPIRITUAL MENTORING WITH HENRI NOUWEN

Introduction

The norm for many of us seems to be that from the moment we wake up, we face a race of activities to be run through: a quick cup of coffee or tea, a shower, maybe getting others ready for the day, eating a light breakfast, nabbing a quick glimpse at the internet to check the news and any messages received overnight, maybe saying a quick morning prayer, and then, like a sprinter, taking off.

Nights are often like a bookend to this experience. After dinner, activities with children or friends, preparations for the next day, maybe some television or reading if time permits, possibly another check or two of the internet, and then before you know it, you're dozing off. Not one more thing is possible—except maybe worrying about what you're going to face tomorrow or unhappily mentally reliving something that happened today.

Life rushes along and carries us with it. It is like we are transported through the day by myriad little things we must do until of course we can no longer do them. We get sick, something happens to change our routine like the dawning of Covid-19, or we die.

Whenever we tell ourselves we need to break through our denial that life is fleeting and fragile so we can change this pattern, we put it off or say it is impractical given all that is on our plate. This is, of course, based on the erroneous belief that we still have time. We will always have time. Henri Nouwen knew such experiences and feelings too. He had been planning a trip to the Hermitage Museum in Russia when he had a heart attack. I feel certain that this would have been a warning sign and experience he would have reflected and written on, but he didn't get the chance. Instead, he had another attack and abruptly died at sixty-four.

Yet Nouwen, despite being like the rest of us in failing to keep a sense of impermanence before his eyes, did take out time to truly live the days he had. He wasn't perfect at it. No one is. But his discipline of reflecting on what is important, and his desire to go deeper in life, made the days as meaningful as possible for him and for us who have the good fortune to reflect on his thoughts now that he is gone.

We need Henri and his wisdom and experience. By embracing the themes he was graced with writing so convincingly on, we can return to our lives each day with different eyes and perspectives. By taking just a few minutes each day in stillness at home or work as we read reflections from his books, letters, and talks we can open ourselves to new possibilities. I have found doing this to be immensely rewarding and freeing, and I continue to reread and open myself to where I am being led, perhaps to places where I might not have gone before.

Maybe his greatest gift is in showing us how to be more centered on what is important, even if only for just a few moments each day. This was Henri's hope and purpose in writing — both for himself and others. What he had to say distilled lessons from life and was steeped in sacred scripture as well as in sound pastoral psychology, which he had studied at the Mayo Clinic.

In what follows you will find opportunities to stop for a few moments, breathe deeply, read and listen to Nouwen, and consider my expansion on his ideas and practices as a way to set the tone for your life. You could use this book to close your day with a desire to be renewed, to redirect your-self back onto the path — or you could use it to start your day each morning, fresh and refocused. Nouwen offers some light in life's darkness so that we might grow more compassionate to others . . . as well as to ourselves.

If you are not yet familiar with the writings of Henri Nouwen, I hope the following reflections will encourage you to go deeper by reading some of his books, all of which are cited in the notes and then again at the end of this book. For those of you who have read Nouwen, or perhaps even knew or personally experienced Henri himself, as I did, my hope is that you will read what is to follow with fresh eyes and experience joy in being reminded of his words. During these challenging times, with hidden possibilities to be re-vealed, we need to hear his voice in our ears, urging us on.

When I shared with my wife, Michaele, the idea of writing a short book on Henri's spiritual guidance, she en-couraged me to do it. She felt that reviewing the material Henri wrote as well as his letters to me and what tran-spired in our two meetings long ago would be good for me as well as for others. She was right. I truly felt evangelized by returning to his wisdom and recalling once again who he tried to be for others with his life.

Nouwen had a strong influence on me, not because he had the answers, but because he could articulate the ques-tions and challenges in such a way that I believed he un-derstood me. He made me feel I wasn't alone in my searching. And so, if the reflections to follow are the "lyrics" of this book, the "music" underlying it is a sense of belonging to a community. *Let's Look Together* is an attempt to help us in our collective search for meaning, for a way to live a rich and compassionate life, and, of most importance, in our search for the God in whom we wish to be centered — especially during these uncertain times.

Henri's openness to the intimacy and personal vulnerability that grounded his caring nature were evident as soon as you met him. This also came through in his books. They were clear, compelling, and (thank heavens!) short enough for the busiest of us to read and reflect on in the midst of our hectic lives. But Henri's ability to be with people was as purposeful in his writings as it was when he met you in the flesh. He wanted to reach out and find a place in others' lives. He longed to be truly present to searching souls looking for something missing at the center. He wanted to have others join him in his personal search for a life that was nourishing, challenging, solid, and real. He truly wanted to be a spiritual friend — a mentor. So in the brief mentoring lessons that follow, we give him the opportunity to do all those things again.

Henri Nouwen

A Brief Biographical Sketch

Henri Jozef Machiel (J. M.) Nouwen was born on January 24, 1932, in Nijkerk, Holland. His parents were Laurent Jean Marie Nouwen and Maria Huberta Helena Ramselaar.

The oldest of four children, young Henri was a dedicated, energetic student. Pious from an early age, priesthood was in his mind from elementary school years. His father, a prominent lawyer, was an accomplished individual, respected throughout Dutch society. He expected the same from his children. Henri's mother was a bookend to her husband in that she was very affirming and encouraging — especially regarding his relationship with Jesus.

The Nouwens were devout Roman Catholics. An uncle on his mother's side was a priest in the Archdiocese of Utrecht.

In 1957, Nouwen was ordained as a diocesan priest and received a degree in psychology from the Catholic University of Nijmegen in Holland. In 1964, he moved to the United States to study at the Menninger Clinic in Topeka, Kansas, and remained there until 1966. His focus, which would be the basis of a lifelong work, was studying the integration of theology and spirituality with psychology. Following this period, he taught psychology at the

University of Notre Dame in South Bend, Indiana from 1966 until he returned home to the Netherlands in 1968 to teach psychology and work on his doctorate in theology.

In 1971, Nouwen returned again to the United States to teach at both Yale (1971–1981) and Harvard (1983–1985) divinity schools. Another turning point in his life was to take a seven-month sabbatical in the 1970s at the Abbey of the Genesee in upstate New York with the Trappist monks and receive spiritual direction from abbot and psychiatrist John Eudes Bamberger, OCSO. In 1981, Nouwen also traveled to Latin America and lived with the poor, an experience that broadened his view of life, revealing to him much suffering and exposing him to violence and fragility for the first time. During his time at the Trappist monastery, Henri had encountered the writings of Thomas Merton, about whom he had written, and his experiences in Latin America left him, like Merton, even more attuned to the issues of social justice. Following this, he accepted an invitation to teach at Harvard. He felt many in Cambridge were over-ambitious and depressed, so the time spent at Harvard was mixed — rich in his own learning and the opportunities he had to share of himself with others. It was, all in all, not a good fit for Henri's soul.

In 1985, at the invitation of Jean Vanier, Nouwen joined L'Arche in Trosly, France, a community for people with developmental disabilities. Eventually, he traveled to Canada and became pastor of their Daybreak Community in Toronto. He wrote of this experience beautifully in a final book called *Adam: God's Beloved*.

Henri Nouwen died suddenly on September 21, 1996, from a heart attack as he was planning to visit The State Hermitage Museum in Saint Petersburg, Russia. He was to visit the Rembrandt oil painting *The Return of the Prodigal*

Son, which Henri had made more famous with a book of the same name.

During his lifetime, Nouwen authored more than forty books which were translated into dozens of languages. Many books of talks and correspondence have also appeared since his death, and several biographies about him. Nouwen's books continue to attract a wide audience because of his ability to write on the spiritual life and psychological challenges all of us must face including rejection, friendship, relevance, compassion, and loneliness. Key to his ability to touch people was his ability to share his own struggles with a unique and personal sense of vulnerability.

I

LOOKING TOGETHER

WITH HENRI NOUWEN

Henri Nouwen
on Living a Rich Spiritual Life

Do not believe that he who seeks to comfort you lives untroubled among the simple and quiet words that sometimes do you good. His life has much difficulty and remains far behind yours. Were it otherwise he would never have been able to find those words.

—Rainer Maria Rilke[1]

The beginning of the spiritual life is often difficult not only because the powers which cause us to worry are so strong but also because the presence of God's spirit seems barely noticeable. If, however, we are faithful to our disciplines, a new hunger will be made known. This new hunger is the first sign of God's presence. When we remain attentive [to it] we will be led always deeper into the kingdom although at times it may not seem it. There, to

---

1. Rainer Maria Rilke, *Letters to a Young Poet* (New York: Norton, 1934), 7.

our joyful surprise, we will discover that all things
are being made new.

—Henri Nouwen[2]

Henri Nouwen was so honest about what a mess
he was. It gives you life, for someone that you love
to say "me too."

— Anne Lamott[3]

To many people—including some of his close friends
and colleagues—Henri Nouwen often seemed to be a
complex, contradictory person. For instance, Carolyn
Whitney-Brown, a former member of the L'Arche Daybreak Community, points this out in a creative, insightful
way:

When I think of Henri, I think of two "books": one
is the book that Henri wrote 40 times, yet couldn't
quite live; the other is the book that Henri lived for
almost 65 years, yet couldn't quite write. The second book waits to be written, as the meaning of
Henri's life and wisdom reveal themselves now,
after his death.[4]

---

2. Henri J. M. Nouwen, *Making All Things New: An Invitation to
the Spiritual Life* (New York: HarperCollins, 1981), 95.

3. From a talk given to The Henri Nouwen Society, Toronto, On-
tario, May 13, 2016; quoted by Tali Folkins in "Henri Nouwen's Gift
to Anne Lamott," *The Anglican Journal* 142, no. 5 (May 18, 2016).

4. Carolyn Whitney-Brown, introduction to the memorial edition of Henri J. M. Nouwen, *The Road to Daybreak: A Spiritual Journey*

This sentiment is certainly true, to an extent, but I think that underneath all of his conflicting surface energy there was also a simple, beautiful man who loved his priesthood, sought to be as honest as he thought he should be, truly cared for others, and wanted to do the right thing with his life and for others. His writing reflects this. His allure was an uncanny ability to take his own specific experiences, feelings, and reflections and then write or speak about them in a way that touched a deep common chord. Most people who read Henri find at least one book that they feel was written just for them.

My feeling about Henri's writings parallels that of singer Dave Alvin's about the folk-composer Kate Wolf. Although Alvin had never met Wolf, he was deeply moved by her song "These Times We're Living In." In the linear notes for the album, he wrote, "I don't know much about Kate Wolf's life and loves, but in a few raw and tender lines, she sure knew a lot about mine."

In his writings and presentations, as well as when we met at Harvard and in Toronto, Henri was able to share feelings that we all experience but seem to elude expression. Most of us often can't seem to find the right words to capture what we're going through, or where we've been. Henri was able to name and describe what we all feel — to shape his words, stand on them, and make more sense of what we are about through them, so that we can spiritually and psychologically go where we must journey in our own lives. That's what I often feel, even today, when I encounter

---

(New York: Image Books, 1990), xii. I am grateful to Michael Ford's *Wounded Prophet*, which points this statement out, and to my friend Brendan Geary for bringing it to my attention again.

Henri's words—especially in his early books—on four themes: *desert wisdom, ordinariness, compassion*, and the interrelated topic of *vulnerability and prayer*.

In addition, the fact that we often don't know where to go next seems more acceptable after reading about Nouwen's own personal confusion and discernments. At a certain level, our struggles don't seem very different from his. When he gets lost, complains, or is petty, we nod and think: *Been there. Done that.* (Or, more accurately, *Am still there, doing that!*) Then, as we move through one of his books, as he gains greater clarity, we seem to gain clarity as well. We experience a wonderful, supportive feeling when his journey toward discernment becomes our own. His spiritual friendship frees us... *mentors* us. It is no wonder that contemporary wisdom figure Richard Rohr referred to Nouwen as a "superb Christian teacher who will surely stand the test of time," and that one of the most widely read spiritual authors of our day, James Martin, SJ, called Nouwen's work, "Timeless wisdom for life from one of the greatest masters of our age."

Simple Kindness... "Let's Look Together"

The desire to care for others was always central to Henri's struggle to discern and be who he could be before God. His spirituality grew out of his vulnerability, and it bore fruit n his kindness. We see it in story after story about him, such as this anecdote shared by Joseph Gallagher, which serves as the inspiration for *Let's Look Together*:

> Henri Nouwen's writing and life were filled with a spirit of simple compassion. Knowing this, a young seminarian about to be ordained sent one of

Henri's little books to an artist friend. He too would soon be ordained.

The young man who received the present was delighted. He took it with him on his pre-ordination retreat in Connecticut. Upon reading it he was struck by one particular line and it gave him an idea.

He decided to go out into the woods and search for just the right stone upon which to paint this beautiful message. This would then serve as a fitting surprise gift for the friend who gave him Henri's book.

As he slowly searched around on the grounds for "just the perfect stone" (as a typical artist would), another retreatant passing by, stopped, and asked him if he had lost something. In response, the seminarian explained his delightful plan to the stranger. Whereupon, the man's face lit up and he said, "Well, I'm Henri Nouwen. Let's look together."[5]

That's what we are doing, here, too. Looking together with Nouwen.

——————

When Henri's book, *The Genesee Diary*, was first released in a mass market paperback edition, he was thrilled that

5. Fr. Joseph Gallagher, "Fr. Henri Nouwen of happy memory," *National Catholic Reporter*, November 15, 1996: 11. This article of readers' memories and appreciations appeared seven weeks after Nouwen's death. Fr. Gallagher was identified as being from Baltimore, MD.

people rushing through an airport might pick up his book for reading on a plane. The convenience of the format made it possible for more people to discover its contents.

Similarly attentive, later in life when he heard from some readers that his book *Life of the Beloved: Spiritual Living in a Secular World* didn't satisfy their yearnings or answer enough of their questions, he was sad and disappointed. He always wanted to reach new groups of people. He wanted to make the spiritual life relevant for all without watering it down into something vague, easy, and magical, something that I think is unfortunately in vogue today.

What was hard for Henri to realize, for example, in the case of *Life of the Beloved* (and in *Making All Things New*, which he also hoped would reach a wider audience), was that he was so centered on a relationship with Jesus that no matter how he tried to cast his work, this came through clearly and powerfully. There was no watering down with him. Henri was in love with Jesus, and could relate to Jesus, in ways that some people simply cannot fathom.

Yet, despite the Christ-centered faith that infused all of his writing, Nouwen's audiences were still much wider than those of many of his contemporary authors writing about Christian spirituality. Although he didn't reach secular people easily, he was enormously successful reaching across the many Christian denominations. One of the reasons for this was his willingness to be "unfinished," to reveal himself to those who listened to or read his words as a fellow struggler. He didn't present as someone who had already arrived. He didn't write from a place of achievement or accomplishment. He knew better than this, and said so—especially when he spoke about the spiritual life:

The battle is real, dangerous, and very crucial. You risk all you have; it is like fighting a bull in a bull ring. You will only know what victory is when you have been part of the battle. People who have tasted real victory are always very modest about it because they have seen the other side and know that there is little to brag about. The powers of darkness and the powers of light are too close to each other to offer the occasion for vainglory.[6]

Vulnerability

When Henri spoke or wrote, his struggles were the most obvious thing that people noted — although, once again, this may not have been his complete intention at the time. While being vulnerable with others was something he wanted and did, he wasn't always aware of how much his anguish was actually out in front of people.

Someone I know and respect once spent a week at Pendle Hill, a Quaker retreat center in Pennsylvania, with Nouwen as a guide. Knowing my belief in, and warmth for, Henri, she shared with me that it was a wonderfully touching experience for her to be with him for a week's retreat. She also said that Henri's sadness seemed to come through so clearly in his conferences that she felt she must let him know how much she appreciated his genuineness and sense of vulnerability. When she told him what she thought, his surprising response was: "Why is it that people are able to see so clearly my sadness, but fail to grasp my joy?"

---

6. Henri J. M. Nouwen, *The Genesee Diary: Report from a Trappist Monastery* (New York: Image Books, 1981), 71–72.

This was a question he was to ask and have to deal with again and again. I think the reality was that he communicated better through his vulnerability and brokenness than through his experiences of love and peace. When you were with Henri, whether across the table or the room, or reading a page of one of his books, you could feel his passion, but—if you were like me—you wished that somehow he would be a little more gentle with himself as well. My hope was that the peace he knew and could find would melt more of his anxiety and impetuous nature so his heart could relax a bit. For example, when we met for the last time, in April 1990, his fingernails were bitten down and he seemed to be running in ten different directions. I sensed in him both a deep holiness and a tense restlessness in him, side by side.

In my letters to him, I would try to be honest and confess my own dangerous impulses to seek comfort instead of a peace that I feared might cost me and others dearly. And in those same moments I would also try to have Henri raise an opposite group of questions for himself, since he seemed to be in a place that was so different from mine. I wanted us both to consider: "Does life with God have to be this hard? Is so much anguish necessary? Must it be this complicated? Do we have to be confronted with our own death to be at peace and let go of the unreasonable self-imposed demands as well as the impossible expectations of others?"

On one occasion, Henri's generous, humble response was to reply simply to me: "Your challenge to live more at peace without having to be confronted with my own mortality is a really important one, and I hear that challenge and want to be very attentive to the questions you raise."[7]

---

7. Personal correspondence, June 18, 1990.

In his own setting at L'Arche (a community of mentally and physically challenged individuals and their companions), where he was chaplain during the last years of his life, he was to be asked to face his restlessness as well. He did so, and wrote and spoke about this poignantly. Then, in 1989, he was hit by a van while walking along the side of the road. He didn't die then. He died seven years later from a sudden heart attack. But he was severely injured as a result the collision with the van. Through all those moments of physical suffering, uncertainty, and emotional pain, he wrote of experiencing much peace. In the book where he related much of this, *Beyond the Mirror*, he also shared how fleeting this feeling was when he got physically well again. In the epilogue to that book he noted:

> It has been a few months since I wrote down my experience in the portal of death. Looking back at it now that I am again fully immersed in the complexities of daily living, I have to ask myself, "Can I hold on to what I learned?"
>
> Recently, someone said to me, "When you were ill you were centered, and the many people who visited you felt a real peace coming from you; but since you are healed and have taken on your many tasks again, much of your old restlessness and anxiety has reappeared." I have to listen to these words.[8]

---

8. Henri J. M. Nouwen, *Beyond the Mirror: Reflections on Life and Death* (New York: Crossroad, 2001), 69.

Facing Rejection

Henri, also like most of us, didn't suffer rejection or lack of attention well. This was another reason his writings come to life for sensitive people like myself who fail to hold onto our sense of identity before a living, loving God when people criticize us. Henri had an uncanny awareness of how quickly his and our moods could be affected — be changed — because of someone else's reaction.

In *The Genesee Diary* and other writings and lectures (some of which are still available on CD), Henri would return to this theme again and again. The following excerpt from his weekly meeting with the Trappist abbot John Eudes Bamberger (his spiritual director for many years) during a 1974 six-month stay at the Abbey of the Genesee offers a sense of his awareness of this in his own life:

> At noon I had another session with John Eudes. I took up the subject of my anger again and explained how often my anger seemed related to experiences of rejection.... In all those cases I didn't just feel a little irritated but felt deeply hurt, so much so that in moments of prayer my thoughts became involved in angry ruminations and revengeful scenes. Even my concentration during my reading got more difficult since practically all my energy went into the experiences of the felt rejection.
>
> John Eudes pointed out my difficulties with "nuanced responses." "The problem," he said, "is not that your feelings are totally illegitimate. ... But the problem is that your response has no proportion to the nature of the event.... Little re-

jections like these open up a huge chasm, and you plunge right into it all the way to the bottom. You feel totally rejected, unloved, left alone, and something like a 'blind rage' starts developing that takes over and pulls you away from concerns and interests that are much more important to you. The problem is not that you respond with irritation but that you respond in a very primitive way: without nuances."

We tried to explore the reason for this fact. Somewhere there must be a need for a total affection, an unconditional love, an ultimate satisfaction. ...John Eudes made it very clear how vulnerable I am with such a need because practically nobody can offer me what I am looking for.[9]

This deep concern with rejection would ultimately reach crisis proportions — ten years later — when an emotionally intimate relationship of his dissolved. Henri was to write about his reactions to this experience in one of his final books, *The Inner Voice of Love.*

Again, I think one of the reasons so many of us feel an affinity with him and his writings is due to his ability to so clearly and convincingly communicate psychological stumbling and spiritual failure. More than that, his own reflections and the helpful reactions of others upon which he reported, teach us about hope, grace ...and *possibility*. We are able to then see the spiritual life as something in process, rather than as a once-and-for-all achievement.

---

9. Nouwen, *The Genesee Diary*, 51–52.

In reading his work we find themes that help orient us, give us peace, and provide a direction toward joy as well. Like Henri, we repeatedly fail, act immaturely, are disappointed in the love we receive, and lose our sense of direction — engulfed in a state from which in the short run we cannot seem to escape. When we read Henri, we are encouraged by the recognition that we are "part of the battle," that we truly are living and flowing with God even in our failures, rather than just existing and drifting in a secular world.

Nouwen was aware of the dual nature of the "inner desert" he felt all people should — must — traverse if they are to experience life fully now:

> The desert — the Egyptian desert of the Abbas and Ammas, but also our own spiritual desert — has a double quality: it is wilderness and paradise. It is wilderness, because in the desert we struggle against the "wild beasts" that attack us, the demons of boredom, sadness, anger, and pride. However, it is also paradise, because there we meet God and taste already his peace and joy.[10]

Henri's attractiveness as a writer remains, not just because he provides clear direction but because when you read his words you know he is with you on the journey.

I always remember that once, when I sent him a copy of one of my books, by return mail he sent me one of his own recently published works. In referring to the title of my book (*Living Simply in an Anxious World*), he wrote at

---

10. Henri J. M. Nouwen, introduction to *Desert Wisdom: Sayings from the Desert Fathers*, translation and art by Yushi Nomura (Maryknoll, NY: Orbis Books, 2001), xvi.

the end of his inscription these two simple words: "I'm trying."

The Spiritual Life

After hearing Henri speak at a conference, a friend of mine had a chance to encounter him closer up when he was moving quickly and anxiously around the hall in preparation for another talk. Later that day she observed to me: "Henri is truly a very holy man." Then, after a pause, she added: "But he is also a nervous wreck."

The next day, I met Henri for breakfast and this bore itself out in a way I found very funny. We had just sat down and opened our menus when Henri abruptly stood up. "This is no good. It is too noisy. They're talking too loudly. Let's move," he said, and bounded off to another table. I took a peek at the two people in an animated discussion at the table next to us. Thank heavens they didn't seem to notice either the outburst or our shift to another table, as they might have taken it personally.

Henri was like many of us in that he often seemed impatient or on the run. People remember this about him, even during times or in settings where it seemed out of place. On one occasion, I remember the silent period of gathering prior to Henri's presentation, when the host who was sitting next to him looked over and saw Henri fidgeting and distracted, impatient to begin his talk. That he is like some of us in his restlessness, however, is only a small part of the story. The transformative part is that he was aware of this, was honest about it, and sought to find ways to understand and respond to it. This approach to a fragmented, anxious, drifting form of existence is what forms for him the structure of what we call "the spiritual life." It

is in the very lack of and hunger for more that Henri's—
and our—hope lies.

In the search for God at the heart of our lives, Henri—
seeking solidarity with his readers—sought to state clearly
the feelings, problems, and results we could expect in the
search as we move from worry to wakefulness, from a
sense of fragmentation to a place of peace and refreshment
deep within ourselves.

In *Making All Things New*, his little classic on responding to God's invitation to live in a more centered, meaningful way, he first helps us recognize our urge to move
more deeply into a relationship with God while simultaneously recognizing that we are confused as to the direction in which we should go. His caution is that we not
merely feel the call to live more deeply and just stop there:

> As long as we have only a vague inner feeling of
> discontent with our present way of being, and only
> an indefinite desire for "things spiritual," our lives
> will continue to stagnate in a generalized melan-
> choly. We often say, "I am not very happy. I am not
> content with the way my life is going. I am not re-
> ally joyful or peaceful, but I just don't know how
> things can be different, and I guess I have to be re-
> alistic and accept my life as it is." It is this mood of
> resignation that prevents us from actively search-
> ing for life of the Spirit.[11]

He believes that this mood can be counteracted by appreciating more deeply the problems that plague us when

---

11. *Making All Things New*, 21, 22.

we are not rooted in the Spirit and open to the buffetings of life. Reflecting on his own busy life, he points out that, even though we move faster and farther, we never seem to catch up to whatever we're chasing. People never seem satisfied with us and we become resentful. We are always planning for the eventualities that we fear will befall us. Meanwhile, our preoccupations with tomorrow don't allow us to enjoy what is before us here and now.

Because our minds and hearts are filled with such worries, we seem to get only fleeting periods of peace within. We are unconnected, alienated, "never at home in our [own] hearts." He recognized this in himself and asked us to ponder with him the realities of our current fragmented life and to seriously consider the question as to what more there might be for us:

> While teaching, lecturing, and writing about the importance of solitude, inner freedom, and peace of mind, I kept stumbling over my own compulsions and illusions....What was turning my vocation to be a witness to God's love into a tiring job?...Maybe I spoke more about God than with him....Maybe I was more concerned about the praise of men and women than the love of God. Maybe I was slowly becoming a prisoner of people's expectations instead of a man liberated by divine promises....
>
> I started to see how much I had indeed fallen in love with my own compulsions and illusions, and how much I needed to step back and wonder, "Is there a quiet stream underneath the fluctuating affirmations and rejections of my little world? Is there a still point where my life is anchored and

from which I can reach out with hope and courage and confidence?"[12]

Henri then came to realize that both his desire and ours to have a strong spiritual center within go deeper. We can see this in his reflection on the attitude of Brother Lawrence of the Resurrection, the seventeenth-century lay French Carmelite whose teachings can be found in the classic treatise, *The Practice of the Presence of God*:

> For Brother Lawrence, to live in the presence of God was his only concern. In the presence of God, life became very simple for him. This simpleness of life, however, was the result of a long struggle.... To be free for God asks for discipline, and... the practice of the presence of God asks for determination to let go from the many worries.... Brother Lawrence's deep conviction that prayer is not saying prayers but [is] a way of living [in] which all we do becomes prayer.[13]

Despite this calling though, most of us are still confused. We don't know what direction to go in, how we can let our knowledge about God become a personal relationship with God. As Henri recognized, we often feel distance from God rather than a Divine sense of intimacy.

While experiencing feelings of alienation from the Spirit of God, we even sometimes look at Jesus through a negative lens. We feel, *Well, of course Jesus had an intimate re-*

---

12. *The Genesee Diary*, 13–14.

13. Henri J. M. Nouwen, foreword to *The Practice of the Presence of God by Brother Lawrence of the Resurrection*, translated by John J. Delaney (New York: Image Books, 1977), 11.

lationship with God the Father and felt the flow of the Spirit between them. After all, Jesus was God! Henri reminds us, however, that in such instances Jesus didn't cling to his identity with God. He became human, had human emotions, and shared his story in human terms so we could see ourselves in him.

Once we dispose of the idea that being intimate with God, as Jesus was, is impossible, Henri then confronts us with a second source of discouragement that comes in the form of preoccupation:

> To be pre-occupied means to fill our time and place long before we are there. This is worrying in the more specific sense of the word. It is a mind filled with "ifs." We say to ourselves, "What if I get the flu? What if I lose my job? What if my child is not home on time? ... " All these "ifs" fill our minds with anxious thoughts and make us wonder constantly what to do and what to say in case something should happen in the future. Much, if not most, of our suffering is connected with these preoccupations....Since we are always preparing for eventualities, we seldom fully trust the moment.[14]

In saying this, Henri sounds to my ear as if he's reflecting one of Mark Twain's wry comments: "My life has been filled with terrible misfortunes...most of which never happened." Even if we are able to recognize what we are doing to ourselves, we live in a milieu so filled

---

14. *Making All Things New*, 25.

with negativity and fabricated emergencies and induced needs that we are convinced we don't have a chance.

Today I think many would agree that when there is no dire news to report, the media searches the world over for sad events, situations that can be dramatized, and anxieties to instill. Simultaneously, people's efforts to do good are portrayed as self-serving, insufficient, and impermanent. In response, Henri proposes the call to the spiritual life as a way to move from worry to wakefulness. Still, he is realistic; his head is not in the clouds. And so he compellingly invites us to face our "homelessness" and offers us a way to come home through the discipline of prayer and community.

Homelessness

To Henri, homelessness was driven by a compulsive concern for the needs of others: "One of the most notable characteristics of worrying is that it fragments our lives. The many things to do, to think about, to plan for, the many people to remember, to visit, or to talk with, the many causes to attach or defend, all these pull us apart and make us lose our center. Worrying causes us to be 'all over the place,' but seldom at home."[15]

Homelessness, for him, also involved a sense of boredom and resentment that arises when we are busy and preoccupied, as well a desire to cover these feelings under a veneer of "niceness." He felt that when we are uncentered and not clear about our purpose or values, our lives seem out of control. The faster we run, the less we feel we ac-

---

15. *Making All Things New*, 36.

complish, the less we feel appreciated. Instead we feel abused and used, and this takes its toll.

Henri's friend and mentor Abbot John Eudes Bamberger once commented on this to Henri. "It is not so surprising that you are easily depressed and tired," he said. "Much of your energy is invested in keeping your hostilities and aggression under control and in working on your appearance of gentleness and kindness."[16]

Henri saw this way of acting as a response to fear of isolation, a fear that drove him to seek the approval of his father and so many others, even though he knew such a quest was unrealistic. Why did he keep at it? What keeps each of us tied to unhealthy ways of living and relating? Acknowledging the distortion, Henri recognized the reality that we need to somehow be part of a meaningful community:

> In interpersonal relations ... [our] disconnectedness is experienced as loneliness. When we are lonely we perceive ourselves as isolated individuals surrounded, perhaps, by many people, but not really part of any supporting or nurturing community ... out of all this pervading loneliness many cry, "Is there anyone who really cares? Is there anyone who can take away my inner sense of isolation? Is there anyone with whom I can feel at home?"
>
> It is this paralyzing sense of separation that constitutes the core of much human suffering. We can take a lot of physical and even mental pain when we know that it truly makes us a part of the life we live together in this world. But when we feel

---

16. *The Genesee Diary*, 81.

cut off from the human family, we quickly lose heart.[17]

Self-Knowledge

Another element of the more self-conscious spiritual life we all desire that dovetails with a deeper sense of community is the call to know ourselves more fully. Henri not only emphasized this but was aware that a critical element of the process of self-knowledge is commitment to discovery of every unfamiliar aspect of ourselves. There are many ways to do this, such as by opening ourselves up to someone we love, or by prayer, reflection, and sharing personal stories with friends, or by being in tune with the feedback we receive each day from those we encounter, or through therapy, spiritual direction, and journaling. These are but a few among many approaches. To be sure, Nouwen used them, and we can see some, but not all, of the fruits of this in his writings.

As we are treated to the process and results of his efforts at self-discovery, though, we must be careful not to jump to the conclusion that all he shared represents all he felt. Otherwise, we will misinterpret who Henri was and, more importantly, we'll be deluded into thinking the process of self-discovery is easier and more straightforward than it actually is.

Of all Henri's books, *The Genesee Diary* is the one that has been the most important on my own journey. Just as I found Thomas Merton's edited journals of life in the Trappist monastery a balm to my soul, so too I found this book

---

17. *Making All Things New*, 32–33.

of Henri's—in its tone, approach, and content—especially reassuring during times of doubt and struggle. There is something about the monastic cadence, spiritual centeredness ("conversion of manners"), and simple honesty that helps put my soul on the right track.

In *The Genesee Diary*, I found the fact that Nouwen's guide, John Eudes Bamberger, was not only an abbot but also a psychiatrist, which was intriguing as well. Unlike many of my colleagues in the mental health professions, Henri's monk-psychiatrist seemed especially clear and direct in his interventions—something I now try to model in as gentle a way as possible in my own mentoring efforts.

It was no accident, then, that when I had my own chance to meet Dom John Eudes I brought up his intervention style. I'd gone to Berryville, Virginia, to meet with my own spiritual mentor, Thomas Merton's final abbot, Flavian Burns, and during our time together Flavian mentioned that John Eudes was visiting and that he'd arranged for us to chat if I would care to meet with him. Naturally, I was very pleased. Not only had I heard about him but also I was interested in his insights on Merton and Nouwen.

After we were introduced, we took a walk in the cloistered area behind the monastery. It was a leisurely stroll during which the former abbot spoke a bit about his own decision to choose a life as a monk rather than a life as a physician. He talked also about some of his impressions of Merton, whom he saw as a truly remarkable man. And he reflected on Henri, whom he viewed with a sharp understanding and gentle appreciation of his human goodness.

At one point, when he paused, I teased him about his style of dealing with Henri as reported by Nouwen himself in *The Genesee Diary*.

"Abbot, I found your interventions to be gentle but surprisingly direct for someone who is also a psychiatrist," I said.

John Eudes stopped, turned, and faced me. Before he spoke, his look seemed to say, *Oh, so you think I was too forthright and candid, do you?* Then he smiled in a mischievous way and said, "One of the monks in my abbey who read *The Genesee Diary* told me that I let Henri off pretty easy. But I told him that I really didn't. It's just that in the published diary Henri left out all the really good comments I made!"

We both laughed.

Henri was more of a psychologist himself than people realized. By this I mean he knew the value of self-discovery and balance when sharing insights about himself. He also knew the need to be painfully honest in looking at his familiar faults and defensiveness. He saw the real value of vulnerability and the danger in believing only the positive traits and impressions people projected on him as a prominent spiritual guide and well-known author.

He saw the importance of sharing his foibles and repeated stumbling efforts with others. He even opened himself to criticism in *The Genesee Diary*, for instance, by allowing people to see the basic challenges and areas where there was some lack of knowledge of certain spiritual practices in his approach to God. This was wonderful for his readers; it allowed us to appreciate that Henri — especially given his accomplishments as a spiritual guide — was still one of us. Given his deep insights and ability to employ the learning that is possible even in taking dead-end journeys in the spiritual life, he becomes then all the more valuable to us.

As Thomas Merton once noted, in the spiritual life we are always beginners, always in over our heads. Echoing Merton, Nouwen gives us the courage to better accept this reality and not get discouraged when we fail again and again.

An element that is also present in *The Genesee Diary*, and that is often overlooked, is his *discretion*. Whereas, people often focus on his vulnerability and seemingly transparent nature, his discretion, another essential feature of his life and work, is under-appreciated. Part of the reason for this is that people undervalue the role that psychology played in the way he approached himself, others, and God. Henri had a knack for sharing just enough of himself and his journey to help people identify with him so they could better explore and understand their own lives. However, he held back from making the mistake made by many spiritual writers of going too far with self-revelation. When a spiritual writer/lecturer/guide does this, the danger is that others will become more centered on the guide than on themselves. Nouwen knew this, and toward the end of his life he even consulted with one of his publishers as to whether in his writing he should share information about his sexual orientation. The advice given to him was that, since he hadn't done so up until that point, he shouldn't, and he listened.

We can learn much from Henri's seemingly natural but actually quite disciplined process of self-discovery and discretion. Brutally honest, eternally hopeful—even during the dark times—he finds value in sharing his experiences, in putting what he has learned at the service of

others. Yet—and this is the careful psychologist in him—
Nouwen shows that all of us need to share our insights
and feelings in a way that is of service to others. With this
simple piece of knowledge, self-discovery can free us to be
even more non-defensive in our prayer, more appropriately transparent when we are called to guide others,
whether we are professional psychiatrists, trained spiritual directors, or just ordinary folks doing the best we can
for others. Without this piece of self-discovery, narcissism
and poor ego boundaries can masquerade as openness,
with little good actually being done for the other person
seeking our support.

A Continuous Bloomer

There is one more special gift that Henri modeled for us
that I would like to mention here. It is that seeing our
"growing edges" (psychologically rough areas, such as defenses, anxieties, rigidity, unexplored gifts, minor signature strengths, and resistance to change that need
attention) is part of the ongoing spiritual process, and
knowing our sins and flaws can actually be a help in developing a deeper relationship with God.

A metaphor from another religious tradition, Buddhism,
teaches about the wonderful possibilities that come about
when we use the "weeds" in our life to make compost to fer-
tilize our interior garden. The belief is that people with real
problems or sins (in Buddhism, *sufferings*) can become truly
holy and compassionate beings. When this happens, their
presence in the world is gracious and grace-filled—not in
spite of their past life but because of it.

I have seen this in counselors and spiritual masters
who were very wounded leaders but didn't run away from

their experiences in the weeds. They walked into their darkness and let it teach them. The darkness didn't lift any faster because of their willingness to be with it. Far from it. The pain, loneliness, and sense of alienation were intense. Yet, eventually the darkness itself became—à la John of the Cross, the Carmelite saint and author of the classic *Dark Night of the Soul*—new light for the next phase of their lives. The darkness itself became the loving face of God leading to new perspectives and clearer life-giving images of God.

Although Nouwen had written books and given public lectures on the spiritual life, those who knew him well sometimes saw his ingrained (what those of us interested in personality psychology might call "characterological") defensive style rear its head. They also saw that even during all of this, God was using him still. And so his value as a guide was not because he had it all together. Instead, it was because he was both humble and hopeful that he was opened to being used by God during these times. And because of what he continued to face—especially during the last ten years of his life—experiences of the weeds and the darkness became important and consistent aspects of his personal witness.

Someone very close to Nouwen felt that although he had many wonderful insights about his life and what it meant to be a true, free person for others, he was in fact a very late bloomer. For example, for most of his life he lived in the shadow of a father with whom he never seemed to feel at ease and loved, although his siblings have shared that they felt their father did his best. But for whatever reason, it just wasn't enough for Henri.

The setting for Henri's early years also didn't help. His father was a formidable, talented, and respected man. Royalty would come to visit him, and scholars would come to consult with him. His personality was quite different from that of Henri's naturally attentive and emotionally present mother. In reaction, Henri sometimes tried to deal with the pull to please and be accepted by his father through achieving great success, all the while knowing in his heart that he should be embracing his ordinariness. I remember how once when I visited him at Harvard he lamented about people who were caught on the ladder of success at the university. "They're all depressed here," he remarked to me. It made him even more convinced that he must let go of all titles and prestige to simply be Henri.

During this visit I also asked for some direction for myself and he helped me more than he ever knew. Amidst his troubles at Harvard (and, as previously noted, possibly because of them), he could understand and connect with me in my own journey toward self-acceptance and self-love. His problems were my problems. His optimism and direction were mine as well. Looking back on that encounter, I feel we were collaborating spiritually in looking at my life even though I could sense his presence in my life at that moment as an *Abba*.

Maybe because of this significant interaction and the simple power and honesty that come through in his writings, I prefer to regard Henri not as a late bloomer, but as a "continuous bloomer." Moreover, I think the spiritual flower within him bloomed most fully prior to his death and that the back-and-forth interaction with his own honest experiences of himself, others, and God give us hope that it is not with a major final breakthrough that we find God. Instead, we are constantly at the shoreline of the kingdom of God, even as the spiral of self-knowledge, self-discovery, and self-love moves back and forth repeatedly throughout our lives.

We are not born again one time, but experience a constant "born again-ness" that allows us to see life as a loving journey in which learning about ourselves, God, and others never ceases. Not to see it this way is to set the stage for much unnecessary discouragement—something Henri experienced in his dark moments and then shared in ways that could help us all reach for God in ways that are enlightening. As Henri tried to teach us, the journey toward God is a grace-filled one we travel—sometimes in darkness, sometimes in light, but always together. He knew the meaning of a collaborative spiritual direction. Because of this, we are all richer for having known him.

II

EXPLORING FOUR SPIRITUAL MENTORING THEMES

WITH HENRI NOUWEN —

AND TAKING THEM A STEP FURTHER

Desert Wisdom

The careful balance between silence and words, withdrawal and involvement, distance and close- ness, solitude and community forms the basis of the Christian life and should therefore be the sub- ject of our most personal attention.

—Henri Nouwen[1]

Desert wisdom initially entered my life in a simple, straightforward way. Then, my subsequent encounters with it were a lot more intriguing and powerful.

I was first introduced to the history, spirituality, and sayings of the fourth-century desert fathers and mothers through the writings of Thomas Merton. His book *The Wis- dom of the Desert* is still the most concise, engaging work on the topic (although for another serious, perhaps more com- prehensive, treatment, read *Word in the Desert* by Douglas Burton-Christie as well). And after Merton, I read Nouwen's *The Way of the Heart*, which Merton's work in- spired him to write. I appreciated Henri's perspective on

---

1. Henri J. M. Nouwen, *Out of Solitude: Three Meditations on the Christian Life* (Notre Dame, IN: Ave Maria Press, 2004), 14–15.

desert spirituality, and told him as much when visiting him at Harvard. Henri immediately responded, "Well, if you liked that book, then maybe you would like this one..." — and reached to retrieve a volume from his shelf: *Desert Wisdom: Sayings from Desert Fathers*, translated by one of his Yale Divinity School students, Yushi Nomura, who added beautiful Japanese brush strokes to illustrate the sayings. Henri was humble. In *Desert Wisdom* Henri wrote: "With his calligraphy and drawings Yushi helped me see more than I had shown him. He became my teacher by making me look at these stories as if I had never seen them before."[2]

As I started reading Henri's introduction to that book later that day, I felt inspired to embrace the Spirit of these desert dwellers even more:

> Who were these desert fathers and desert mothers? They were men and women who withdrew themselves from the compulsions and manipulations of their power-hungry society in order to fight the demons and to encounter the God of love in the desert. They were people who had become keenly aware that after the period of persecutions and the acceptance of Christianity as a "normal" part of the society, the radical call of Christ to leave father, mother, brother, and sister, to take up the cross and follow him, had been watered down to an acceptable and comfortable religiosity and had lost its converting power.[3]

---

2. Henri J. M. Nouwen, introduction to *Desert Wisdom: Sayings from the Desert Fathers*, translation and art by Yushi Nomura (Maryknoll, NY: Orbis Books, 2001), xiii.

3. *Desert Wisdom*, xiv.

But then, for whatever reason, I set desert spirituality aside.

Sometimes we aren't ready to see how to integrate something so powerful and important into our daily life and routines. That was true for me until a friend and colleague, a Jesuit priest, Bill Sneck, called on September 21, 1996, to tell me that Henri had died. Henri was in The Netherlands when it happened. He'd suffered a fatal heart attack.

I was stunned and saddened. I hung up the phone and went to the basement to look over all of Henri's books on my shelves, especially some that he had signed for me. Included in these was that copy of *Desert Wisdom,* the book he had given me when I visited his little apartment near Harvard Square. He'd written that day:

To Robert J. Wicks
In grateful memory of your visit
Joy and peace
Henri J. M. Nouwen
April 9, 1984

I thought, *Why had I forgotten my deep love for the "spirit of discipleship" of the desert fathers and mothers?* And then, in Henri's honor, I asked myself, *How could I now use them more completely to help guide me?* They had so much to teach—those desert dwellers, and Henri too. How might I also integrate this hard-won wisdom with psychology and other spiritual traditions in order to show others ways to open up, let go, and be free to flow, rather than merely drift along in life? How might these fathers and mothers help me learn to guide others?

Nouwen's beloved take on the desert wisdom of the fourth and fifth century calls us to appreciate the "purity of heart" that's available at each stage of contemporary life whenever and wherever we are. It means learning better how to be present, prayerful or mindful, clear, and kind.

We can see these qualities most clearly in little children. They have a sense of wonder. Once, when my oldest granddaughter Kaitlyn was quite young, she called out early in the morning to her mother. Since we were visiting and sleeping right across the hall from her, my wife went in to see what she was calling about. She told me that when she entered the room, Kaitlyn had her head in her hands, elbows leaning on the windowsill, with her eyes looking out the window, up at the sky as the sun rose. When she turned and saw her grandmother entering the room, she turned back again at the window and pointed up and said with great energy, "Look Mommom! God is coloring the sky again."

Like the desert fathers and mothers, who were true sages, children who have the right type of spiritual modeling also are exceedingly kind. A priest I know was once sitting with his niece at an elementary school event. After it was over, the children started to leave, class by class. When his niece's class had its turn to exit, one of the little boys said to the priest: "Do you want to leave with us so you're not sitting here by yourself?"

Also like the desert fathers and mothers, children have a sense of simplicity before society has a chance to complicate their view of life. The story that fits this depiction for me is of a child who unexpectedly returned home late from school one day. Her mother, understandably worried over this, said to her when she entered, "Where were you?!" The little girl looked a bit surprised at her mother's reaction and replied, "Oh, I stayed a bit to help a classmate who was in trouble." Now, her mother was surprised and asked, "Well, what did you do for her?" To which the little girl said simply, "I sat down next to her and helped her cry."

Nouwen knew and shared directly in *The Way of the Heart* how, with a little attention, some discipline (and the sense of simplicity we see in children), it is possible for us to experience purity of heart more often than just at special times. Reflecting on desert wisdom, he recognized that we must be focused if we wish to find the pearl of great price. He was following the lead of Thomas Merton, who put it this way:

> Happiness consists in finding out precisely what the "one thing necessary" may be, in our lives, and in gladly relinquishing all the rest. For then, by a divine paradox, we find that everything else is given to us together with the one thing we needed.[4]

Knowing this simple truth is part of the wisdom that the desert teaches us.

Our challenge is to absorb this knowledge and recognize the freedom it presents when we live with God truly at the center of our lives—not in artificial or only in compartmentalized "Sunday religious" ways. Instead, we need to integrate autonomy (our will) with theonomy (God's will). While this is never easy, it is possible—even simple—and powerful, but only if we are willing to open ourselves, make the effort involved, and then "let go." We have been given the grace to come this far. The choice about what to

---

4. Thomas Merton, *No Man Is an Island* (Boston: Shambhala, 2005), 137.

do in response is *ours*. We can begin by appreciating how the desert can teach us the importance of silence, solitude, and unceasing prayer.

Just as Merton's desert spirituality was not confined to the one book he specifically wrote on the topic, Nouwen's sense of this spirituality and thoughts about it were not limited to *The Way of the Heart*. The book does, however, crystalize how the *amma*s and *abba*s of the fourth and fifth century impacted his spiritual core, especially in terms of the three themes of silence, solitude, and unceasing prayer. Nouwen recognized that we need to "fashion our own desert where we can withdraw every day, shake off our compulsions, and dwell in the gentle healing presence of our Lord."[5]

Both *Desert Wisdom* and *The Way of the Heart* were the fruit of a course Nouwen had taught at Yale Divinity School. In his own words, "It was one of the most stimulating seminars I have ever been part of." Both the original course and those books were designed to fathom ways in which the early Christian spiritual pioneers had something to say to us today — particularly those who are involved in reaching out to others.

Henri was worried about the state of ministry in churches. Much later, during the height of the Covid-19 pandemic and its variants, his words came back to me again in an even stronger way: "Many of us have adapted ourselves too well to the general mood of lethargy. Others among us have become tired, exhausted, disappointed, bitter, resentful or simply bored. Still oth-

---

5. Henri J. M. Nouwen, *The Way of the Heart: Connecting with God through Prayer, Wisdom, and Silence* (New York: Ballantine, 2003), 30.

ers have remained active and involved — but have ended up living more in their own name than in the Name of Jesus Christ."[6]

In response to this, he recalled early desert father Arsenius's formative encounter with God that led him into the wilderness. It was a wilderness he felt all of us must enter in this way, too.

> Arsenius prayed again: "Lord, lead me in the way of salvation" and again he heard a voice saying, "Arsenius, flee, be silent, pray always, for these are the sources of sinlessness." The words *flee, be silent,* and *pray* summarize the spirituality of the desert. They indicate the three ways of preventing the world from shaping us in its image and are thus the three ways to life in the spirit.[7]

Nouwen was inspired as well by the *Apophthegmata Patrum,* or "Sayings of the Fathers," because he felt they provided "spiritual commentaries...counsel to visitors, and...very concrete ascetical practices" worthy of reflection today.[8] The *Apophthegmata Patrum* is the original Latin collection of stories and sayings upon which every study of Christian desert spirituality is based. For Nouwen, the admonition to Arsenius to flee meant the critical need for some solitude, which Nouwen felt was "the furnace in which transformation takes place" for each of us.[9] It is also

6. Nouwen, *The Way of the Heart*, 12.
7. Nouwen, *The Way of the Heart*, 15.
8. Nouwen, *The Way of the Heart*, 14.
9. Nouwen, *The Way of the Heart*, 20.

the place where the desire to help (compassion, kindness, generosity, ministry, caregiving) is fed by our spiritual core. In other words, a true sense of perspective requires time alone.

Solitude and Silence

Henri felt that when most people speak of solitude they really mean a desire to be left alone, a "place" where they can mentally complain, have the freedom to do what they want, and have a sense of privacy. Truth be told, the desire for these things is more therapeutic than spiritual. For example, in the case of the *ammas* and *abbas* of the desert, the goal was *metanoia*, which literally means "repentance" or "change of heart" and implies a true sense of letting go and conversion. Henri also appreciated that while time in solitude was beneficial, it wasn't ever easy.

From a psychological perspective, I remind people that when they sit in silence and solitude they create an emotional vacuum. And, as all of us remember from our high school science classes, nature abhors vacuums — even psychological ones! As a result, the preconscious — or from a cognitive perspective, those ways of thinking, perceiving, and understanding we do not want to examine — rises to the surface and there we face our embarrassments, angers, shame, and other negative projections and self-incriminations that we have tried to avoid.

Henri knew this. In his own words:

> In solitude I get rid of my scaffolding: no friends to
> talk with, no telephone calls to make, no meetings

to attend, no music to entertain, no books to distract, just me—naked, vulnerable, weak, sinful, de-
prived, broken—nothing....As soon as I decide to
stay in my solitude, confusing ideas, disturbing fan-
tasies, and weird associations jump about in my
mind.[10]

In our solitude we are offered the gift of being
wrapped in gratitude to God. We are in a place where we
are able to step back from secularism's values. In place of
fame, greed, competition, and the other demons of non-
Gospel values, we are able to encounter a God of love who
will call us to allow the Spirit to "make all things new"—
including, especially, ourselves.

However, simply being alone will obviously not open
us to this. *Silence* is also necessary.

Henri once described an experience he had during a
drive through downtown Los Angeles. He reported having
the sensation of driving through a "huge dictionary."
Wherever he looked he saw signs trying to convince him to
buy something, use something, *possess* something that
would make life more enjoyable and comfortable. He felt
that in all this verbiage, there was no real respect for
words; they were useful only for manipulation—not for
turning people to what was truly good. In contrast, in the
desert, the *abba*s and *amma*s had such respect. They realized that freely used words could be the source of sin,
serve to dissipate our sense of mindfulness, and result in
cheapening our messages. In *The Genesee Diary*, Henri reports an experience that reinforced these concerns:

---

10. Nouwen, *The Way of the Heart*, 27.

Silence. Indeed, silence is very important for me. During the last week, with a trip to New Haven [where he taught at Yale at the time] full of discussions and verbal exchanges, with many seemingly necessary telephone conversations, and with quite a few talks with the monks [at the abbey of the Genesee], silence becomes less a part of my life. With the diminishing silence, a sense of inner contamination developed. In the beginning, I didn't know why I felt somewhat dirty, impure, but it dawned on me that the lack of silence might have been the main cause.[11]

While discussing silence, he goes to the heart of the matter — which is the silence within. In desert spirituality this was central, and it led to a deep concern with unceasing prayer. For Nouwen, unceasing prayer was a possibility, in fact, a discipline that had the power to affect one's whole life. Unceasing prayer was realistic to achieve, and could be felt through one's own:

- simple kindness (because Nouwen recognized that time in silence and solitude softened his soul in the same, albeit lesser, way as it did for St. Anthony, one of the *abba*s who spent twenty years in isolation in the desert)

- appreciation of interpersonal pain and rejection (because these feelings surfaced during his alone time)

---

11. Henri J. M. Nouwen, *The Genesee Diary: Report from a Trappist Monastery* (New York: Image Books, 1981), 133.

- understanding of what the so-called "spiritual life" is (because Nouwen knew that he needed to have God at his side when facing his own demons)

- awareness of the inner homelessness many of us experience at times (because during quiet prayer he had no place to run for distraction)

- deep appreciation for the importance of true self-knowledge as well.

Through the practice of unceasing prayer, Nouwen learned what the desert fathers and mothers knew: that the battle is never over, the journey is endless, the learning never stops, the possibilities for ongoing understanding of ourselves and of the way we are being challenged to embrace grace is endless. As reform theologian Rudolf Bultmann would say in his lectures: "Grace can never be possessed but must be received again and again." This truth is, I believe, behind all of Nouwen's writings, not simply those in *The Way of the Heart*. His writings contain words that both satisfy and challenge...always call us to more...and invite God to make all things new, including us.

Taking Nouwen's Words Further:
Let the Desert Teach Us

As Merton's and then Nouwen's words about the desert experience moved me, I set out on my own journey, mindful of the visual image and spiritual perspective provided by the desert. My hope is that you will do the same in your own ongoing journey.

There are stark physical attributes of real physical deserts, as journalist William Langewiesche explains in *Sahara Unveiled*. The desert is "the earth stripped of its gentleness, a place that consumes the careless and the unlucky. ...The Sahara has horizons so bare that drivers mistake stones for diesel trucks, and so lonely that migrating birds land beside people just for the company. The certainty of such sparseness can be a lesson. I lay in Algiers in a hotel in a storm, thinking there is no better sound than the splash of rain."[12] Now, translate this visceral, physical experience with your spiritual journey. With these words one can see the essential core of the deprivation providing an opportunity to value simplicity, friendship, and prayer. It is in this very atmosphere of "nothingness" fed by silence and solitude that we encounter our own emotional and spiritual deserts where we are given the opportunity to re-evaluate our lives and potentially experience anew true inner freedom for a while.

So when we find ourselves on an inner desert journey, who better to turn to for guidance than the ancient disciples of the desert and their contemporary counterparts who have physically and/or spiritually entered into these barren areas, only to emerge with wisdom to share? They learned to live more simply, gratefully, and completely. As Nouwen explains so well, so too can we. With their guidance we can be released from unnecessary worries and useless tendencies to travel down fruitless paths; we can be freed to experience joy, peace, and compassion.

---

12. William Langewiesche, *Sahara Unveiled: A Journey across the Desert* (New York: Vintage, 1997), 7.

The fourth-century Christians drew inspiration from Moses, Elijah, John the Baptist, and Jesus, who were all desert dwellers before them. These prophetic figures knew much about what lies at the core of life. *Amma*s and *abba*s were true spiritual apprentices who appreciated the need to let go of whatever might be squeezing the air out of life either spiritually or psychologically. They were also able to welcome that which would replenish the soul and foster inner freedom by helping them see what needed to be let go of so the journey would not be inordinately burdened by attachments. Their goal was to *seek only what was essential*, knowing the rest of life would then fall into place.

Ask most people today what they want—especially in the midst of a pandemic, world strife and violence, and each day's uncertainties—and the reply is often very simple: a little peace and joy. In their search for peace and joy, some shuttle from spirituality to spirituality hoping to find what matters. Others dig in their "psychological heels" and pull dogmatic theological tenets over their heads in an effort to shield themselves from change and insecurity. Their fantasy is that these supposed "anchors" will offer the security they desperately desire—but they never do.

The ancient group in the desert, however, saw the world's insecurities and lack of values in their own time as a wake-up call to let go of what was causing the anxiety. For them, being troubled wasn't simply the result of encountering something disturbing that needed to be conquered or removed so they could return to what is now referred to as the "normal." Instead, they had the spiritual wisdom and psychological maturity to see anxiety as merely an easy-to-spot signal, a new opportunity to gain perspective to determine or rediscover what is essential.

A healthy perspective has long been held in high esteem by mental health professionals. And at the same time when the *ammas* and *abbas* of Christian antiquity were seeking wisdom in the desert, Jewish scholars and ancient rabbis of the Talmud who were also seeking wisdom advised: "You do not see things as they are. You see things as *you* are." Buddhists speak of the wisdom sought as "the unobstructed vision," and Hindus in the *Upanishads* consider it as a "turning around in one's seat of consciousness." In the New Testament, we also hear Jesus say, "If your eye is healthy, your whole body will be full of light" (Mt 6:22).

We too should strive to seek this wisdom. We can see life differently by cultivating the main virtue of the desert: humility. This is important, because when we take knowledge and add humility, we get wisdom. And when we take this very wisdom and add it to compassion, we get love — and God is love. The desert fathers and mothers would refer to this as "purity of heart," which, according to Thomas Merton again, is a "clear unobstructed vision of the true state of affairs, an intuitive grasp of one's own inner reality as anchored, or rather lost, in God through Christ."[13]

Dynamically oriented psychotherapists interested in unconscious forces may seek to approximate a version of this awareness of clarity by helping their patients make the unknown known. They seek to enable them to become conscious of their resistances to change, develop good self-

---

13. Thomas Merton, *The Wisdom of the Desert: Sayings from the Desert Fathers of the Fourth Century* (Boston: Shambhala, 2004), 7.

knowledge based on an increased awareness of what were once hidden unconscious forces, and reach a level of maturity at which they have what is referred to as "a less fractious ego." Despite the help psychology can provide us in our search for inner freedom, purity of heart in the spiritual sense requires more than cognitive insight or emotional maturity. It involves a true *conversion*, the fruits of which include the inner peace of letting go of unnecessary worry and attachments by opening ourselves to God in a new and radical way.

But before we can follow in the path of those who have sought and found the freedom that accompanies purity of heart, we must first be honest and humble enough to appreciate that we are not free now. How are we not free? Humility must be at the very core of our outlook, attitude, or perspective. We need to take a cue from Abba Anthony, a father of the desert, who tells us, "I saw all the snares that the enemy spreads out over the whole world and I said, groaning, 'What can get me through such snares?' Then I heard a voice saying to me, 'Humility.'"[14]

In addition, we need not only to see ourselves for who we are—in terms of both our gifts and growing edges or defenses—but also to take the actions necessary to let go of what has captured our hearts, preoccupied us unnecessarily, and made us insecure and anxious.

To seek the freedom that humility offers, we first have to appreciate that our vision is not clear now. Instead, although we may be unaware of it, our soul is heavy, and our psychological arms are full of much that is unnecessary and harmful to our sense of simplicity and peace. We

---

14. Benedicta Ward, *The Sayings of the Desert Fathers: The Alphabetical Collection* (Collegeville, MN: Cistercian Publications, 1984), 7.

need to become aware of, and possibly even disgusted by, this reality. When we do, we will know deep in our hearts that there is a serious need for unlearning and for emptiness. This is essential if we are to welcome the fresh wisdom that will set us free from the cultural and unconscious chains that are quietly binding us. As Douglas Burton-Christie writes of John Cassian, one of the early fathers of the church, and a theologian who was formed by the desert, "The problem with the old learning was at least in part psychological: it prevented the mind from absorbing the new ethos of the Scriptures....There was a clear sense among the educated ones who came to the desert that learning would have to start over in this place."[15]

But how do we start over? More specifically, what are the essential questions we must ask ourselves if we wish to let go of all that is unnecessary in our desire for purity of heart? Many questions can be posed in response to this, but there are four central ones that I believe all of us who wish to be "desert apprentices" must confront as the seekers did in the fourth century. We need to do this if we truly wish to let go of everything that is troubling and misdirected in ourselves so we can be free—not just free for ourselves, but for those who count on us as well.

Such freedom does not mean that we will never be without pain, uncertainty, fear, or a sense of being lost at times. What the desert journey does mean, though, is that being free from the common, yet unnecessary, suffering that

---

15. Douglas Burton-Christie, *The Word in the Desert: Scripture and the Quest for Holiness in Early Christian Monasticism* (New York: Oxford University Press), 158.

overshadows our days can often be avoided; so, in its place, we can open space for creative and generous pursuits.

For some, the concept of letting go is truly an attractive concept. Yet, in honestly answering the questions that follow, we can learn that while the concept may be basically simple, it is still not easy to live. At each step of the way and each stage of life, our challenge will be to recall the question: *Am I still truly serious about seeking what will free me?* It is not that we are called to be psychological pyromaniacs setting fire to anything that offers the simple pleasures of life. Instead, in scriptural terms, we are called to be clear about what the pearl of great price is (see Jesus' parable in Matthew chapter 13) and truly willing to pay for it.

Once when I was in Corpus Christi, Texas, for a meeting, I met a former student of mine. He now had a leadership position, and I was interested in how he was faring in this new role. He suggested we meet for dinner, so later that night we sat down for a wonderful meal and great conversation. During dinner he surprised me by saying, "I'll never forget one of the points you made in class." Intrigued, I asked him what point I'd made that had such an impact on him. He smiled and replied, "You told us that we could have peace if we wanted it. Then, after a short pause, you added, 'as long as that was *all* we wanted.'" I appreciated hearing this again. I myself needed the reminder. True passionate intent that leads to action is obviously quite different from mere fantasy that results in only words and no lasting commitment.

The call of the spiritual desert is begun by pausing to consider things that maybe for years we have wistfully thought about but in reality have ignored, skirted, or run away from. In our desire to be truly centered we could begin by asking ourselves: *What fills me now?* We may have to grapple with our answer to this. It is not an easy question to face, because we have become so accustomed to much in life that's unnecessary or has taken too prominent a role in our lives. These things have unconsciously or — in some cases — more clearly become a ransom that must be paid if we are to be happy.

Most of us don't even know this is the case. As the Chinese proverb goes: "He has too many ticks to feel the itch." Yet, if we ask the right questions of ourselves, we can better discern where it is we're holding onto something less than God or God's will.

In our effort to identify our inordinate attachments, we could ask ourselves:

- Where and on what do I spend most of my free time, energy, and emotions? What do I worry about? It was Jesus who said, "For where your treasure is, there your heart will be also" (Mt 6:21).

- When do I become self-absorbed in a way that may lead to moodiness and a short temper? For some people, this happens so often they don't realize it; for them, every third Tuesday might be a dark night of the soul.

- Do I recognize that sometimes I can become so fixed on my self-image that I'm unwilling to face myself to become free? When I questioned a colleague one day about his motives, his face got red, he grew angry, and he said, "*Never* question my integrity!" But it is by constantly questioning our own integrity that we can learn when and how we have fooled ourselves—and being very emotional is a good sign that we have.

As we seek purity of heart, another question that might be helpful is: *What prevents me from letting go?* Often what prevents us from letting go, from seeing ourselves clearly, is that we take detours down four psychological cul-de-sacs: projection, when we blame others; self-condemnation, when we treat ourselves in a harshly judgmental, punishing way; and discouragement, when we don't receive immediate positive results.

In addition to these three, there is a very insidious block to our being able to let go that often comes as a "friend": a sense of entitlement that masquerades as justice. In other words, the sense of *I deserve this.* Frequently underlying all these obstacles to letting go is—once again—a lack of true humility, as Nouwen reminds us. Discovering how petty, selfish, and inappropriately self-interested we are (because there is also a healthy form of self-interest) becomes too difficult because we truly don't believe at our core that we are loved by God.

And then there is another question, a vexing one, but perhaps the most important question of all: *What is "the one thing necessary" that I should embrace and with which I should fill myself that will satisfy, yet simultaneously and paradoxically help me remain open for more once "the room is swept clean"?* There is no single answer to this *koan*—a puzzle for which there is no simple right or wrong answer—but the following points may be helpful.

- One powerful way to empty ourselves of un-necessary needs and quiet avarice is by embracing a deep sense of gratefulness. When we do this, a false sense of neediness becomes less of a problem.

- Another way is to both simplify and become less scattered so that we can be more centered on what is truly important in our life now. As novelist James Joyce quipped in *Dubliners*, "Mr. Duffy lived a short distance from his body." Our culture and our ego distract us and seduce us to become busier, which is quite different from simply being active. Being active is a mindful action. Being busy is draining, because we are always preoccupied with how we look, whether we are succeeding, or if we are doing better than others.

- Yet another way to embrace the one thing necessary is to be open to seeing life differently, because purity of heart requires that we be receptive to other views and change. After my mother died at the age of ninety-five, I said to my daughter that she had had a full life but she tended to be negative at times. My daughter's response was: "I don't think Grandma was as unhappy as you feel she was. I just think she wasn't happy in the same way you and I are." (Wisdom from the young, if we are open to it.)

- And one more aid that fosters a search for, and valuing of, purity of heart, is a recognition of the proximity of death. Thomas Merton once wrote in his journal that while at prayer he had felt the angel of death passing him by without stopping, but that he sensed he had taken notice of him. This had a deep impact on him. Nouwen also changed, albeit temporarily, after his first heart attack in Russia when he felt he had been facing death.

A final approach I have found helpful, one in which we can paradoxically fill ourselves yet remain open, is unceasing prayer. Letting go and finding the one necessary thing doesn't just happen. It takes awareness, prayer, and action. When we pray and metaphorically or actually take our seat in the center of the room to pray, we can count on "visitors" from our memory or preconscious (awareness lying just below the surface) to visit us. This requires us to be appropriate hosts to them as the *ammas* and *abbas* were before us. They did not seek to inordinately entertain these visitors by focusing on them. They also did not totally ignore or run away from them. Rather, in the silence and solitude of their cells, they compassionately noted these cognitions (ways of thinking, perceiving, and understanding) so they could understand what—whether from their egos or the world—was taking attention away from that one essential thing—living and sharing life fully as God had gifted them to do.

When they did this, their lives became less defensive and more spacious, and their center of gravity was moved from what was unnecessary to what was life-giving. The depth of their quiet time was, as Nouwen would refer to it, a "nest" to which they could return during the day. And the wonderful result was that they could become lighter and more friendly with themselves. This also had a wonderful and freeing indirect impact on those who walked with them in some way, for, as Nouwen aptly notes, "it is from [the] transformed or converted self that real ministry flows."[16]

Mentoring Moments...

(Quotes from Henri Nouwen to provide an opening for you to reflect on the theme of desert wisdom)

> By entering into the Egyptian desert, the monks wanted to participate in the divine silence. By speaking out of this silence to the needs of other people, they sought to participate in the creative and recreative power of the divine Word.
>
> Words can only create communion and thus new life when they embody the silence from which they emerge. As soon as we begin to take hold of each other by our words, and use words to defend ourselves or offend others, the world no longer speaks of silence. But when the word calls forth the healing and restoring stillness of its own silence, few words are needed: much can be said without much being spoken.
>
> (*The Way of the Heart*, 57)

> Abba Poemen said: "A man may seem to be silent, but if his heart is condemning others he is babbling ceaselessly. But there may be another who talks from morning till night and yet he is truly silent."
>
> (*The Way of the Heart*, 64)

---

16. Nouwen, *The Way of the Heart*, 20.

Looking me right in the face with his great eyes [Brother Elias] added, "Don't worry about how to speak about the Lord. When you allow him to enter your heart, he will give you the words."

(*The Genesee Diary*, 20)

I am not saying... there is an easy solution to our ambivalent relationship with God. Solitude is not a solution. It is a direction. The direction is pointed to by the prophet Elijah, who did not find Yahweh in the mighty wind, the earthquake, the fire, but in the still small voice; this direction, too, is indicated by Jesus, who chose solitude as the place to be with his father.

(*Clowning in Rome*, 28–29)[17]

---

17. Henri J. M. Nouwen, *Clowning in Rome: Reflections on Solitude, Celibacy, Prayer, and Contemplation* (New York: Image Books, 2000).

Ordinariness

Here lies hidden the great call to conversion: to look not with the eyes of my own low self-esteem, but with the eyes of God's love.

— Henri Nouwen[1]

When you live outside yourself, it's all dangerous.

— Ernest Hemingway, *Garden of Eden*

Henri Nouwen told me, when he was at Harvard, that from then on he wanted to be known simply as "Henri." To be candid, I thought at the time, *Sure, you publish with Doubleday and Harper. You have studied at the Menninger Clinic and taught at Notre Dame, Yale, and Harvard, so now you have the freedom to be simple.* But, out of respect—since he was the mentor—I kept these thoughts to myself. A discussion about such issues would best be left to his meetings with his spiritual director, Dom Eudes Bamberger, the abbot of the Abbey of the Genesee.

Later, I discovered the struggle he had had with "ordinariness," for he spent his whole life trying to please, first,

---

1. Henri J. M. Nouwen, *The Return of the Prodigal Son: A Story of Homecoming* (New York: Image Books, 1994), 99.

as a young boy, his father, and then others throughout his adult years. Nouwen's need to impress people became clear in his writings and what he shared with, and demonstrated to, those who knew him well. It wasn't a hidden need, and that was one of the beautiful gifts Henri gave to others who crossed his path in person, as well as in his writings and presentations. People who were disappointed in him for not becoming "extra-ordinary" I think missed the major call that he had to articulate, the call to conversion, to allow the Spirit to make all things new. Whether we get there the way we want, when we want , is irrelevant to the whole journey we take in humility, which is the central gift of the the "desert fathers and mothers" of the fourth and fifth centuries.

As I mentioned earlier, I think Henri wrote *The Way of the Heart,* as well as the introduction to Yushi Nomura's book of calligraphy, because of what had been kindled in him by first having read Thomas Merton's *The Wisdom of the Desert*. In that profound work, the Trappist monk wrote:

> These monks insisted on remaining human and "ordinary." This may seem to be a paradox, but it is very important. If we reflect a moment, we will see that to fly into the desert in order to be extraordinary is only to carry the world with you as an implicit standard of comparison. The result would be nothing but self-contemplation and self-comparison with the negative standard of the world one had abandoned. Some of the monks of the desert did this, as a matter of fact: and the only fruit of their trouble was that they went out of their heads. The simple men who lived their lives

out to a good old age among the rocks and sands only did so because they had come into the desert to be themselves, their *ordinary* selves, and to forget a world that divided them from themselves. There can be no other valid reason for seeking solitude or for leaving the world.... They knew that they were helpless to do any good for others as long as they floundered about in the wreckage. But once they got a foothold on solid ground, things were different.[2]

This is worthwhile for all of us to recall as, while wrapped in gratitude before God, we enter silence and solitude to open up a space where autonomy (our will) and theonomy (God's will) might become one. We too can have ordinary desert experiences with, and of, God.

In what I believe to be one of his finest books, *The Return of the Prodigal Son,* Nouwen concerned himself again with the theme of ordinariness. *The Return of the Prodigal Son* is interesting in terms of its history. It surprised some when it came out in 1992 because in the previous years Henri had published what some would term fairly "light" books dealing with piety (although they did help many people). When one of his publishers was asked about the difference, Nouwen indicated that *The Return of the Prodigal Son* had actually been started much earlier and was long in coming. In part a reflection on a famous painting but also on one of Jesus' most famous parables, the book is simply stunning.

---

2. Thomas Merton, *The Wisdom of the Desert: Sayings from the Desert Fathers of the Fourth Century* (Boston: Shambhala, 2004), 25.

One of his goals in writing it was to unveil what he felt were the "seductive" voices that say, "Go out and prove that you are worth something." He said that Jesus was also led to the desert to hear voices to prove he was worth being loved only if he could show he was successful, popular, and powerful. Nouwen then admitted that "those same voices are not unfamiliar to me. They are always there and, always, they reach into the inner places where I question my own goodness and doubt my self-worth."[3]

He then went on to admit that he often caught himself dreaming about being wealthy, famous, or powerful in some way. In reflecting on this, he noted that, "All of these mental games reveal to me the fragility of my faith that I am the Beloved One on whom God's favor rests. I am so afraid of being disliked, blamed, put aside, passed over, ignored, persecuted, and killed, that I am constantly developing strategies to defend myself and thereby assure myself of the love I think I need and deserve. And [using the imagery of the biblical parable of the Prodigal Son] in so doing I move far away from my father's home and choose to dwell in a 'distant country.'"[4]

According to the parable of Jesus recorded in Luke chapter 15, a younger son chose to leave his father's home. Instead of appreciating the true freedom he already had, he decided to take off and spread his wings. In a different way, the older son—who was a good and dutiful person—was not residing in his father's true home because he didn't have the right attitude; he'd also left home, but in a spiritual way. He lacked true love.

---

3. *The Return of the Prodigal Son*, 36–37.

4. *The Return of the Prodigal Son*, 37–38.

Nouwen was to confess in *The Return of the Prodigal Son* that it was the older son whom he felt represented a danger that was far more perilous. He could identify with this type of person and it upset him deeply. He wrote:

> Isn't it good to be obedient, dutiful, law-biding, hardworking, and self-sacrificing? And still it seems that my resentments and complaints are mysteriously tied to such praiseworthy attitudes.... At the very moment I want to speak or act out of my most generous self, I get caught in anger or resentment. And it seems that just as I want to be most selfless, I find myself obsessed about being loved. Just when I do my utmost to accomplish a task well, I find myself questioning why others do not give themselves as I do. Just when I am capable of overcoming my temptations, I feel envy toward those who gave in to theirs. It seems that wherever my virtuous self is, there also is the resentful complainer.[5]

In another book, *The Inner Voice of Love,* Nouwen would again mention Rembrandt, the artist who painted *The Return of the Prodigal Son*—Nouwen's inspiration and muse for the earlier book. And he would use Rembrandt, as well as Vincent Van Gogh, as models of people who were not led astray from their vocations but faithfully lived them. He mentions that as soon as these artists recognized their talents (what some of us might refer to as "charisms," mentioned in 1 Corinthians chapter 12), they focused on

---

5. *The Return of the Prodigal Son*, 70.

who they were being called to be and become. They trusted their unique vocations and didn't seek to become pleasers. In being true to their vocations they were even willing to pay the price of poverty, and they left the world the fruits of their faithful response. Nouwen recognized that he needed to be more like these two artists in following his own calling, rather than searching for unconditional love where it could not be found.[6]

Taking Henri's Words Further:
Recognizing That True Ordinariness Is Tangible Holiness

Jiddu Krishnamurti, the famous mid-twentieth-century teacher of Eastern philosophy, in his book *Life Ahead*, suggested that, in trying to be a person other than who you really are meant to be, your mind wears itself out. As we can see in the lives and words of the desert fathers and mothers — and in the life and writings of Henri Nouwen — recognizing the need to simply be yourself and not fall prey to a culture of greed, power, and preoccupation with one's image and achievements is not easy. Every desert dweller knows about the illusion of control, and realizes that security based on anything less than trust in God is pure folly. He or she also understands and embraces the belief that the humility of the desert — what we might call "ordinariness" — combined with sound practical knowledge can lead to true wisdom.

---

6. See, for example, Henri J. M. Nouwen, *The Inner Voice of Love: A Journey through Anguish to Freedom* (New York: Image Books, 1999), "Stop Being a Pleaser," 5; and "Come Home," 12.

Desert dwellers' commitment to what is true and good led them—and leads us, today, who seek to follow the same path—to spare no effort in our search for self and for God. A commitment to live more authentic lives drives us to let go of current social norms and follow uncharted ways to find and embrace the truth. When we succeed in doing this, our lives become transparent and in that transparency we are able to offer others a pure space, uncontaminated by insecurity, self-interest, pride, or any other number of inner "demons," as the *abba*s and *amma*s called them, that are often left unnoticed and unexpelled from people's lives. The *abba*s and *amma*s were people without guile, transparent, *free.* Unlike much of the world then—and now—desert dwellers are not held captive by worldly values, anxieties, or fears; they, perhaps more than any other group we could learn from, appreciate the beauty and freedom of ordinariness. This was surely a major reason why Nouwen was so drawn to them.

The desert fathers and mothers asked for the grace to let go of the illusions and delusions upon which their identities had previously been based. They wanted only to discover how to be themselves—to be ordinary. This is what Henri wanted, too. Along the way they discovered that the journey into the desert was just the beginning. The longest and most difficult journey was the journey inward.

Centuries later, the Carmelite sister, reformer, and author of classic works of Christian spirituality, Teresa of Avila, taught that we find God by uncovering our own true selves, and it is in the search for God that we can better discover who we are. This appreciation for ordinariness enabled St. Teresa, like those earlier mentors, to experience the sacred, within herself and in God. Contemporary psychologists—my colleagues—describe it as having healthy self-esteem. Persons who have healthy self-esteem are not dramatically swayed by the opinions or reactions of others but are willing to look at their actions and cognitions in response to the feedback they receive.

Throughout the centuries there have been followers of Jesus who were willing to go out from the noise and distractions of the city to hear the word of God, to encounter temptations (see Mt 4:1–11, Mk 1:12–13, Lk 4:1–13), and to "come away to a deserted place" all by themselves "and rest a while" (Mk 6:31). As Thomas Merton recognized, the flight of the early Christian pilgrims to the desert was "a refusal to be content with arguments, concepts, and technical verbiage." Instead, "They sought a God whom they alone could find, not one who was 'given' in a set, stereotyped form by somebody else."[7]

Even though, as Nouwen would emphasize again and again, simply being yourself is not easy, experiencing the freedom and joy of simply being yourself is wonderful—not only for you, but for those you encounter. We can see this in photos taken of people being truly spontaneous. We can particularly notice this in the case of children, and we hope they can retain this quality by continuing to develop their unique gifts and talents rather than succumbing to the needs and pressures of the crowd. In the words of poet E. E. Cummings in a letter to a friend, "To be nobody-but-yourself—in a world which is doing its best night and day to make you like everybody else—means to fight the hardest battle which any human being can fight; and never stop fighting."[8]

---

7. Merton, *The Wisdom of the Desert*, 5, 4.

8. *E. E. Cummings: A Miscellany*, ed. George J. Firmage (New York: Liveright, 2018), 364. This is from "A Poet's Advice to Students."

Even when the uniqueness of a person is welcomed for who that person is—not simply who or what we would want them to be—the process of self-discovery must continue. Recognizing and letting go of masks and flowing with one's natural and developed gifts and talents can be confusing. This is especially so at the beginning of the search for our simple, unvarnished ordinary selves. It is not surprising, then, that this is one of the initial major goals of being in a therapeutic, coaching, or mentoring relationship, or when participating in some type of psychological or spiritual search—to identify masks, and work on letting them go.

Psychological and spiritual journeys can (and perhaps *must*) also be at times disconcerting. One of the reasons for this is that there are periods of transition from who we thought we were to who we are learning we are. Still, the twists and turns of confusion melt at certain points, and then we can see more clearly and know that the journey of self-discovery is worth it.

Fathoming our self—our ordinary, unvarnished self as it almost magically unfolds—is also a key part of the ongoing creative work of every person. In one of the passages from *Letters to a Young Poet,* Rainer Maria Rilke advises his junior correspondent—and us today:

> If your daily life seems poor, do not blame it; blame yourself, tell yourself that you are not poet enough to call forth its riches; for to the creator there is no poverty and no poor indifferent place. And even if you were in some prison the walls of which let none of the sounds of the world come to your senses—would you not then still have your

childhood, that precious kingly possession, that treasure of memories? Turn your attention thither. Try to raise the submerged sensations of that simple past; your personality will grow firm, your solitude will widen and will become a dusky dwelling past which the noise of others goes by far away.

What Rilke is pointing out is that studying and embracing ordinariness is like taking an un-self-conscious inner journey. The goal is not to reinvent ourselves into someone who we innately are not. It is to embrace the heart of our talents and face our foibles and growing edges without recrimination for who we are not—nor may ever be. Such an interior spiritual pilgrimage includes undertaking psychological journeys to different parts of ourselves that haven't fully seen the light of day. This is needed so that the minor signature strengths and virtues we have can be more readily acknowledged, claimed, developed, and shared. After all, we can't take responsibility for an emerging fuller sense of self—the person we are called to be by God—if we don't know (or only vaguely suspect) it exists.

Adolescents naturally take this journey as they explore what is psychologically probable about themselves. Given the fearful forces that surround many young people, the choices they make are sometimes not in keeping with an exhilarating calling to self-exploration because they don't feel loved. This is one of the reasons Nouwen kept emphasizing the importance of viewing ourselves as "the beloved" in God's eyes. In fact, submission to the "other," represented sometimes by society or family pressures, can be deadly to the fulfillment of a dream embraced in early years — namely, the prizing and flowering of who we really are.

Our interpersonal environment will often play down or resist our identity, our being and becoming who we uniquely are. As we've seen, Nouwen experienced and wrote about this. In response to this common danger, Roger Housden, in *Ten Poems to Change Your Life,* cautions, "Whatever your circumstances, people will start to give you advice as soon as you disturb the status quo. That advice is likely to be bad. It will be bad because they are seeking, not to understand further your calling, but to preserve the world as they know it."[9]

Being ordinary today is to act in a countercultural fashion. In a world clearly mesmerized by "spin," narcissism, exhibitionism, and image-making, the spiritual journey instead centers on humility and discernment as to who God is calling us to be. This can change in emphasis at different points in life — even if we feel we are at peace where we are. Certainly Abram was well situated when he was called to strike out to become Abraham, the "father of his people." Similarly, his wife Sarai had grown comfortable being barren and knew the physical dangers of becoming pregnant at her age — especially in biblical times. Yet, she was willing to become Sarah, a woman filled with new potential (see Genesis chapter 17).

---

9. Roger Housden, *Ten Poems to Change Your Life* (New York: Harmony Books, 2001), 9. To read further on this from a psychological vantage point, see Stephen Joseph's book, *Authentic: How to Be Yourself and Why It Matters* (London: Piatkus, 2016) and my own *The Tao of Ordinariness: Humility and Simplicity in a Narcissistic Age* (New York: Oxford University Press, 2019).

Ordinariness gives us both a spiritual and a psychological vantage point from which we can recognize and embrace our real talents, as well as their limits instead of fantasizing about them. The reason for this is that once we accept both our gifts *and our limits*, the opportunity for growth and depth will seem almost limitless. Prior to that acceptance, much of our energy can be wasted on seeking to be someone or something we are not in order to attract and please the (often imaginary) crowd around us. In such a case our existence is spent in front of a virtual mirror. We need to leave the stage of secular society to simply and hopefully live out life in our own reality in the company of others who wish to follow God and do the same.

Austrian-born Jewish philosopher Martin Buber points to the call to be ordinary in a way that echoes the Christian theme referred to as *imago Dei* (being made in the image and likeness of God). This teaching of Buber's from the Hasidic masters illustrates how we are each called to be truly ourselves, nothing else or "more":

The maggid [preacher] once said to his disciples:
"I shall teach you the best way to say Torah. You must cease to be aware of yourselves. You must be nothing but an ear which hears what the universe of the word is constantly saying within you."[10]

When we let go of ourselves, we can be open to "what the universe of the word is constantly saying" within us, we can connect with clarity to God.

---

10. Martin Buber, *Tales of the Hasidim* (New York: Schocken Books, 1991), 107.

Nouwen struggled successfully throughout his life, but not without pain as a writer and as a human being, continuing to call himself to recognize this essential spiritual tenet: the beauty and importance of ordinariness. He did it by addressing the need for, and value of, humility, self-respect, simplicity, and the kind of contemplation in which *kenosis* (an emptying of self of what was not of God) could take place.

For us, too, the virtue of ordinariness is about moving our lives from a daily focus to protect, project, and build up our image to an approach that is more like a journey or pilgrimage in fullness and inner freedom. Being ordinary results in the opportunity to offer "interpersonal space" and compassion to others so that they can feel a similar freedom to accept and become more themselves as well.

Once when Archbishop Desmond Tutu was speaking to a group of seminarians at General Theological Seminary in New York City one of the seminarians in the audience nudged the dean who was sitting next to him. When the dean looked over at him, the student whispered, "Desmond Tutu is a holy man." In response, when the dean asked the seminarian how he knew this, the student didn't bat an eye but immediately said, "I know that Desmond Tutu is holy because when I am with him, *I* feel holy."

Maybe we know it when we see it. Ordinariness is an attitude or stance that allows people to explore and be intrigued by current realities and possibilities within themselves. It is marked by a comfort with oneself that leads to appropriate transparency. Essential aspects of enhancing the understanding and expression of personal ordinariness include the courage to confront unhelpful external influences (even those coming from people who purport to have one's best interests at heart); the true humility to honor one's talents while clearly and gently viewing one's shortcomings in an honest, nonjudgmental fashion; and a willingness to embrace and model lack of egoism in one's personal relations in ways that would encourage personal freedom in others and thus to become more fully ourselves.

To embrace ordinariness, I imagine we all must pass through three psycho-spiritual "gates." If we wish to be open to and benefit from all we experience — including the painful psychological, physical, and spiritual deserts — we must learn to walk through each one. If we don't, we consign ourselves to an existence that is one of merely going through the motions each day. We perform the tasks — possibly admirably — but while focusing on the details of life (what we need to do), we miss the larger picture (the gift of life, *our* life) given to us by God.

The first gate is a passionate commitment to finding out who we are and what our charism (gift from God) is. In appreciating what it is and how we can develop it further, we discover that our efforts are not dimmed by failure because our passionate commitment is not based on success. Instead, it is fired by faithfulness and a spiritual sense of awe for what life can be when it is touched by courage, openness, and gratitude for all we have been given.

The revered rabbi, Abraham Joshua Heschel, had such a sense of spirited passion. It pervaded his life and even his journey at the end of life. This is evidenced in the following story told by his former student and longtime friend, colleague, and fellow rabbi, Samuel Dresner:

> Several years before Abraham Heschel's death in 1972 he suffered a near fatal heart attack from

which he never fully recovered. I traveled to his apartment in New York to see him. He had gotten out of bed for the first time to greet me, and was sitting in the living room when I arrived, looking weak and pale. He spoke slowly and with some effort, almost in a whisper. I strained to hear his voice.

"Sam," he said, "when I regained consciousness, my first feelings were not of despair or anger. I felt only gratitude to God for my life, for every moment I had lived. I was ready to depart. 'Take me O Lord,' I thought, 'I have seen so many miracles in my time.'"

Exhausted by the effort, he paused for a moment, then added: "That is what I meant when I wrote [in the preface to my book of Yiddish poems]: 'I did not ask for success; I asked for wonder. And you gave it to me.'"[11]

Now, that is a life of passion!

The second gate is knowledge. True knowledge can shield us from unnecessary mistakes in nurturing our inner life, as well as the lives of our family members, friends, and others who seek our help when they are lost, confused, or in a "spiritual desert." Motivation is important, but it is not enough. Passion certainly helps us to start the car and be open to the adventure of the trip — but it also helps if we know how to drive.

---

11. Samuel Dresner, ed., introduction to *I Asked for Wonder: A Spiritual Anthology*, by Abraham Joshua Heschel (New York: Crossroad, 1986), vii.

Even the most sensitive and self-aware individuals can miss so much. I remember a talented psychologist approaching me once in the hallway at the university where I was teaching to ask if we could chat for a moment. We went into my office, I closed the door, motioned for him to sit down, sat down across from him, and asked, "What's up?"

He then related how he was having problems with colleagues, friends, and even his own children, who would roll their eyes when he started to share his woes. Because of this, he said that he had decided to re-enter therapy; he hadn't been in therapy since he had been in training to be a psychotherapist himself.

I told this colleague that as a friend I was glad he was going to treat himself to some time to reflect and have the support of being on the receiving end in a therapeutic relationship. I also commended him for his courage in doing this.

"Courage?" he responded. "Yes," I said. "I feel that when we enter therapy it provides a safe place where we can feel free to be ourselves and know that it will be all right. The therapist can best help us see what it is we are doing that is making situations worse or preventing them from becoming better. When we are feeling bad about situations, we often want someone to tell us that we are fine and the world needs to change. But that doesn't really help. That's not where the power is, and it takes courage to face this reality."

I am reminded again of how Abbot Bamberger, a trained psychiatrist, spoke to Henri Nouwen as his spiritual director in ways that helped Nouwen withdraw his projections of blame onto the world while also not condemning himself. In this way Nouwen could gain a healthier perspective on what he was facing in life that he found discouraging.

Although ordinariness seems to be an easy virtue to embrace, it can be at times a precarious undertaking. Looking at today's world of hype and narcissistic self-display, simply embracing our ordinary self sometimes feels like standing alone in the middle of a field and seeing a summer storm quickly gathering in the distance. As you stand there you can see a black wall of rain smoothly sweeping toward you, but you're not sure what to do. Staying in the middle of the field is not safe if it is an electrical storm. And even if it isn't, you know that by standing still you certainly will wind up getting soaked. Should you run for cover under a nearby tree? By running for cover, you might stay dry, but if lightning hits the tree you may also end up dead. And if you try to seek protection in a safe place down the road, you might never make it in time to avoid being soaked by the rain. None of the options seem sensible or attractive.

Trying not to think about how we can further understand or express our ordinary self is not the answer either. Yet, many of us feel we are at an impasse or in darkness, given how simply being ourselves seems so countercultural in a world that is going in the other direction. We may not be able to prevent life's chilling storms, but we must do what we can if we want to create a fuller narrative. This will require a willingness to uncover and face the unnecessary darkness we ourselves may be producing through a lack of self-awareness, self-acceptance, and self-love; our tendencies toward dishonesty, intolerance, and irresponsibility; ignoring unfinished business or addictions; suppressing negative feelings; refusing to deal with insufficiently surfaced embarrassments and unacknowledged greed.

While uncovering and facing all these things, we need to learn to gently laugh at ourselves. When people enjoy themselves and can get in touch with their own beauty, they can even reach the point of teasing themselves. Henri did this well, even at times playing the fool. This can be a wonderful way in which people can free themselves to be more open to others instead of being overly protective because of low self-esteem. Developing a sense of humor about themselves allows them to enjoy their recognition of their foibles. We have all known people like this and it is worth emulating them. For instance, one of the most impressive things about Merton, according to Dom John Eudes Bamberger, was his ability to laugh at himself during the darkest of times. He sought to not take himself too seriously so that there was space to take God and the welfare of others seriously instead. This is real wisdom.

Desert wisdom helps us to differentiate between unnecessary suffering and the kind of pain that must be faced rather than defended against or avoided. Good knowledge, like healthy food, is necessary for living. Each day we need to strive to live by the principles of appropriate self-care and respect and maintain a healthy perspective.

The third gate, unsurprisingly, is *humility.* It is the narrowest gate of all. Humility is the ability to fully appreciate our innate gifts and current growing edges in ways that enable us to learn, act, and flow as never before. Prior to this important passage we may be drained by defensiveness or wandering in our own desert, chasing a false image of self that has nothing to do with who we are really called to be by God.

We usually know that at some point that we need to go through the gate of humility. Knowing is not the problem. The problem is that we are often unaware of the fact that we have actually stopped being humble and, in the process, lost our sense of perspective and gratitude. If we are lucky, something wakes us up—sometimes even rudely—to face this. The following story shared with me in verse by a Franciscan priest (who desires to remain anonymous) illustrates the point quite well:

> I had a dream that death
> Came the other night,
> And Heaven's gate swung wide open.
>
> With kindly grace
> An angel ushered me inside;
> And there to my astonishment
> Stood folks I had known on earth
> And some I had judged
> And labeled unfit and of little worth.
>
> Indignant words rose to my lips,
> But were never set free;
> For every face showed stunned surprise,
> Not one expected *me*.

With humility, knowledge is transformed into wisdom, and that wisdom then ultimately leads us to open up new space within ourselves where we can experience freedom and love. Humility allows us to be appropriately transparent. It is for this reason that it's so important. A great deal of unnecessary worry and stress can be avoided if we treasure this gift. Many of the dialogues and stories told by the *amma*s and *abba*s of the desert illustrate this. The stories are told from the vantage point of people totally dedicated to living a full, meditative life of inner peace, humility, and unselfconscious compassion — something we should all be striving for.

In all of these teachings, humility leads us to honor our ordinariness so that we can:

- seek, feed, prune, and share our unique voice by appreciating it more deeply in prayer, discussion with friends, and focusing on the fears or past training that distort or muffle this voice;

- take greater risks in exploring potential gifts we may not feel we have but others have noted in us and encouraged us to share;

- be stimulated to take greater risks in exploring potential gifts or lesser signature strengths that require courage to display and use;

- expand our tolerance for failure and looking foolish; sometimes we will fail and look foolish as we fathom ourselves and our talents, as well as our unnecessary fears and anxiety; after all, it is silly to grimly hold onto the side of the pool when we could swim in the ocean with a smile on our face.

Humility is also an essential ingredient in life because it leads to *kenosis*, an emptying of the self — the very desert spirit of letting go about which Henri so eloquently wrote and spoke. At its core, humility creates space in our lives for:

- simplicity amid the complex demands of personal and work life

- pacing ourselves while resisting the constant lure of speed and technology

- gratefulness and giftedness in a world filled with entitlement

- enhanced honesty and clarity, instead of spinning the truth to our own advantage

- real relationships in place of manipulations of others to have them fill our needs the way we want them to

- restraint instead of instant gratification and aggression

- doubt and a willingness to ask deeper questions rather than filling ourselves with false certainty and pat answers

- reflection, so that compassion doesn't lead to undisciplined activism

- generosity instead of strident self-interest

- transparency in areas where opaque defensiveness is our norm

- self-respect in lieu of inordinate self-doubt or unbridled self-assurance

- willingness to examine our actions and motivations so we don't wander down blind alleys of projecting blame onto others or condemning ourselves

- forgiveness, so that we don't fall prey to rigidity and self-righteousness on the one hand, or feel this means we need to submit to what we believe is wrong on the other

- willingness to always be authentic, rather than being caught up in what is currently in vogue.

- the courage needed to be ordinary instead of wasting time chasing after what we believe will make us special in the eyes of others.

It is the ability to empty ourselves that creates new inner space in our lives for the surprising and remarkable gifts of humility.

Humility can be encouraged in us as well by the example of the courageous people who came before us. For me, Henri Nouwen, Flavian Burns, and a handful of other significant mentors have taught me to strive with all my might to be simply myself. As I've hopefully made clear by now, this is not a green light for egoism or self-centeredness. Instead, it is a matter of *becoming one's self*, as the rest of nature seeks to only be itself. In doing this we discover how to better flow with life, and this ability to flow should open doors in us so that we can help others as well.

As I've learned from Henri and developed in a personal retreat on ordinariness, the following points are essential for considering in silence and discussing with a mentor or treasured friend. You may use these in your life.

Ordinariness is an attitude of living and reflecting on ourselves in ways that help us seek to...

- embrace the true humility that comes from knowing our own gifts and appreciating our own growing edges, weaknesses, and challenges with a sense of equanimity,

- see life clearly as it is, not as we might wish it to be,

- embrace the call to be who we might become while accepting where we are at the moment,

- move toward accepting all of life — including sadness, questions to which you have no answers, and unwanted feelings and the thoughts and beliefs underpinning them that you haven't examined as fully as you should,

- offer others the space to be themselves as well,

- question the reputation we currently have with ourselves so it can open up a larger and more accurate self-narrative that we are the author of, rather than give this responsibility over to society, family history, past trauma, or unexamined rules,

- find the crumbs of silence and solitude already present in our life so we can relish living into them,

- challenge the needs we say we have or the ones others say we *must* fill in order to be happy,

- value pacing and timeliness over haste,

- become more aware of what we are experiencing in the present moment,

- avoid jumping to conclusions and unnecessary judgments about ourselves and others,

- honor a spirit of "unlearning" so that we can be our ordinary self in the now rather than be held captive by what might have been helpful in the past but doesn't apply today,

- reject an egoistic way of viewing the world as revolving only around us,

- avoid making comparisons with others that are not helpful,

- gain a more appropriate sense of transparency that comes from being a person without guile so that we can help psychologically and spiritually purify our inner and interpersonal environment as much as possible,

- examine the stories we tell ourselves about our lives, and if some of these stories aren't accurate or helpful, look for alternative stories that will be encouraging and challenging,

- welcome other truly ordinary people to accompany us on our journey while maintaining a willingness to open similar interpersonal space for others,

- categorize ourselves and others less so we can be open to understanding more deeply who we and others are,

- celebrate our uniqueness and the difference of others, and look for how others may be teaching us new ways of self-understanding and appreciation of the world,

- avoid the dangers of extreme self-doubt on the one hand and inordinate self-confidence on the other,

- be more in touch with, and able to self-regulate, our emotions,

- not waste energy on pleasing others, but be willing to be compassionate and empathic without expecting anything in return,

- recognize that becoming more aware of our own personality strengths and personal joyful pursuits is essential and worthwhile,

- desire not simply to "fix" what is wrong with ourselves, but instead to build on the positive aspects of our ordinary self,

- develop a mission statement and ethic of living that flows with an appreciation of our ordinary self, not the dictates of others,

- examine the feedback we have gotten that was helpful as well as that which was off-putting,

- enjoy being with ourselves and growing comfortable in laughing at ourselves, instead of being defensive,

- appreciate what people and situations make life more joyful and meaningful,

- know better the signature strengths we have so we can share them more effectively with others,

- contemplate what we would like written on our epitaph,

- develop an ability to be *intrigued* by yourself, as you might be by someone you admire who has a sense of simplicity, humility, inner freedom, courageousness, yet ordinariness about them.

As I look back on my work in the areas of resilience, self-care, compassion, and maintaining a healthy perspective—over forty years of being a psychotherapist, mentor, and clinical supervisor of helping professionals—there are questions that I wish I would have asked. They are almost all questions about one thing: *releasing*, or what I have thus far referred to as "letting go." Maybe I didn't ask such questions because, in pacing a session, they didn't seem appropriate. Possibly, as I walked with people at a turning point in their professional or personal life journeys, I felt the question would ask too much of them — and maybe that was sometimes true. In my own life, these questions may not have surfaced because I was afraid of where they might lead. But no matter the reasons, the end result was the same: I think that I and others experienced less inner freedom and perhaps a failure to fully fathom the amazing paradox that can come with "letting go."

Today, I would refine my belief and practice even further, to say that the most important thing we can do for ourselves and the world around us is release what is not of us so that we can enjoy our ordinary selves and share ourselves freely with others. Learning how to do that is what I believe to be the central importance of this book as well. The time for rediscovery of the virtue of ordinariness by all of us is now.

I remember once delivering a presentation to a packed room of nine hundred people at a large conference that had attracted more than twenty thousand participants. Afterwards, a young woman who appeared to be in her early twenties patiently waited at the end of a line of people who had questions for me. When her turn came, instead of asking for further clarification or following a strand of something I'd said, she began with, "Your presentation wasn't what I expected." Then she added, "Somehow, I thought you would talk down to us. Instead, you spoke about yourself, shared stories and ideas. You walked *with* us." I was moved by her words. I knew that, at least in this instance, ordinariness and transparency, as well as my faith in those listening to my words (rather than simply expecting them to have trust in me), had come across. My voice seemed to have encouraged, in at least this one other person, a "space" in which to better find her own. I wish this happened every time — the creation of a space between people seeking to simply be themselves turns into a circle of grace in which everyone benefits. This is another description of what Nouwen called "living compassion."

Mentoring Moments...

(Quotes from Henri Nouwen to provide an opening for you to reflect on the theme of ordinariness)

"Look at Rembrandt and van Gogh. They trusted their vocations and did not allow anyone to lead them astray. With true Dutch stubbornness, they followed their vocations from the moment they recognized them. They didn't bend over backward to please their friends or enemies. Both ended their lives in poverty, but both left humanity with gifts that could heal the minds and hearts of many generations of people. Think of these two men and trust that you too have a unique vocation that is worth claiming and living out faithfully."

(The Inner Voice of Love, 33)

"There is within you a lamb and a lion. Spiritual maturity is the ability to let lamb and lion lie down together. Your lion is your adult, aggressive self. It is your initiative-taking and decision-making self. But there is also your fearful, vulnerable lamb, the part of you that needs affection, support, affirmation, and nurturing.

"When you heed only your lion, you will find yourself over extended and exhausted. When you take notice only of your lamb, you will easily become a victim of your need for other people's attention. The art of spiritual living is to fully claim both your lion and your lamb. Then you can act assertively without denying your own needs."

(The Inner Voice of Love, 78)

"I think that most of my fatigue is related not to the type of work I do but to the false tensions I put into it."

(The Genesee Diary, 57)

Compassion and Community

More important than any particular action or word of advice is the simple presence of someone who cares.

— Donald McNeill, Douglas Morrison,
and Henri Nouwen[1]

As long as we are lonely, we cannot be hospitable because as lonely people we cannot create free space. Our own need to still our inner cravings for loneliness makes us cling to others instead of creating space for them.... When we think back to the places where we felt most at home, we quickly see that it was where our hosts gave us the precious freedom to come and go on our own terms and did not claim us for their own needs. Only in a free space can re-creation take place and new life be found. The real host is one who offers that space where we can listen to our own inner voices and find our own personal way of becoming human.

---

1. Donald P. McNeill, Douglas A. Morrison, and Henri J. M. Nouwen, *Compassion: A Reflection on the Christian Life* (New York: Image Books, 2006), 13.

But to be such a host we have to first of all be at
home in our own house.

—Henri Nouwen[2]

I once sent Henri a manuscript prospectus for a book I
was writing that was tentatively titled *Relationships: Relish-
ing the Gift of Availability*. When I met with him later to talk
about the idea, he shared a strong feeling about it as soon
as we sat down in his apartment off Harvard Square.

"I looked over your proposal," he said. "You seem
more practical than this. For most of us, 'availability' is not
just a gift but more often a problem." Then he added,
"There must be something from scripture that reflects what
I'm talking about."

"What is it?" I said.

"I don't know," he said, waving a hand in the air.

After we had spoken a while longer about this, and
also generally about life and work, he suddenly interrupted me in mid-sentence, exclaiming, "I've got it! The
theme from scripture is *pruning*. When you prune something, it doesn't blossom less, it blossoms more deeply."

I'll never forget this encounter. What an impact it had
on my life. He was so right. Sometimes we need to prune
in our quest for more compassion and community in our
lives.

Henri's concern about compassion came through
clearly in his own book, which I've quoted many times already, *The Inner Voice of Love*. Here's another quote from
that book: "Only when you are able to set your own

---

2. Henri J. M. Nouwen, *Reaching Out: The Three Movements of the
Spiritual Life* (New York: Image Books, 1986), 101–2.

boundaries will you be able to acknowledge, respect, and even be grateful for the boundaries of others."[3]

And still more quotes:

> When your call to be a compassionate healer gets mixed up with your need to be accepted, the people you want to heal will end up pulling you into their world and robbing you of your healing gift. But when, out of fear of becoming a person who suffers, you fail to get close to such people, you cannot reach them and restore them to health.[4]

> Giving without wanting anything in return is trusting that all your needs will be provided for by the One who loves you unconditionally.[5]

> When you get exhausted, frustrated, overwhelmed, or run down, your body is saying that you are doing things that are none of your business [or to my mind, when you are doing them in ways that are costing unnecessary energy].[6]

Henri and his two co-authors were to speak more about this in *Compassion: A Reflection on the Christian Life.* The need to be more discriminating in how and when we should be available to others is essential. This is not only for our sake, but also for the sake of those who depend on

---

3. Henri J. M. Nouwen, *The Inner Voice of Love: A Journey through Anguish to Freedom* (New York: Image Books, 1999), 9.

4. Nouwen, *The Inner Voice of Love*, 45.

5. Nouwen, *The Inner Voice of Love*, 65.

6. Nouwen, *The Inner Voice of Love*, 67.

our ability to reach out to them. I have found that one of the greatest gifts we can share with another person is a sense of our own peace, and we can't share what we don't have! It is as simple as that, and we can hear it in Henri's words of caution:

> When we are no longer able to recognize suffering persons as fellow human beings, their pain evokes more disgust and anger than compassion. It is therefore no wonder that the diary of Anne Frank did more for the understanding of human misery than many of the films showing long lines of hungry faces, dark buildings with ominous chimneys, and heaps of naked, emaciated human corpses. Anne Frank we can understand; piles of human flesh only make us sick.[7]

He knew the need for compassion as well as its dangers. His lifelong proclivity to psychologically "burn out" taught him that taking great care in being present to others is essential. Yet he also found it hard to turn down requests and then worried about whether his response was good enough. He was so very human!

I still remember him saying "No" to me once when I made asked him to write something in a book I was editing. He spent a good deal of time excusing himself when he could have simply said he was overwhelmed at the time and left it at that. I would have understood and easily accepted the simpler response.

One of the things I found particularly impressive in Nouwen as a mentor was that rather than simply letting

---

7. McNeill, Morrison, and Nouwen, *Compassion*, 54.

the challenges he faced be a cross for himself, he was able to recognize them as problems many of us also face. Although he had a hard time limiting his own work and not feeling it always had to be original and admirable, he guided people like me who feel we must say "yes" in every instance and also must perform notably in what we do. I was to see this behavior again later on.

One morning over breakfast in Toronto at a conference at which we were both speaking, I told Henri that I had attended the keynote presentation he had given earlier. Immediately, he wanted to know what I felt about what he had done and started unpacking his reasoning for it, explaining that he had wanted to create by engaging everyone in an active way. In his presentation he had involved members of the L'Arche community who had intellectual disabilities. They came out into the audience and handed out bread that he had broken at the podium. It was a dramatic demonstration of the theme of his talk: "take, break, and share ourselves."

Although I did stay for the Mass that followed, my thinking at the time was that I really didn't need to attend the "official Eucharist" that was to follow because I had already received God within me. It was a living message of who we should be and who we should become as a result of receiving the body and blood of Christ in the Eucharist and sharing it. The presentation and actual distribution of the bread by members of L'Arche would come back to me again when I read the words of Benedictine monk and liturgist Godfrey Diekmann: "What difference does it make if the bread and wine turn into the Body and Blood of Christ and we don't?"

In sharing with me his hopes for the presentation and curiosity about my reaction, which is natural, I could also sense Henri's desire for affirmation that what he was doing was good, maybe exceptional. And so, in his mentoring of me that morning, he was also (probably unconsciously) modeling vulnerability about his own fears and concerns.

Growing up caught between an overly reserved father and a loving mother who demonstrated what compassion and love look like in the flesh was so very exhausting for Henri. Thinking about his experience made me reflect as well on how my own background and needs affected the way I lived and responded to others. It made me reflect further on what my stated mission in life was and whether it was really being lived out in a spirit of love. We all need these corrections, these reminders, these affirmations.

The encounter with Henri that day was both rewarding and instructive. As I look back on it now after all these many years, his lessons and lived example instructed me more than those of people who always present themselves as having achieved the pinnacle of holiness and wisdom. As I was called upon later in life to guide others who sought to be available to people as mentors, but were often themselves burning out in the process, I recognized the need for them, as well as me, to continually prune what we do. For instance, as I reflect on Nouwen's own gift and pain in reaching out, I share with others a simple paradigm. You are welcome to use this, if you can. If someone asks you to help in some way, consider the following approach:

1. If it seems to be something you are definitely called to do, say yes.

2.   If it is something you know is certainly not what you feel called to do, politely decline.

3.   If it is, as is most often the case, something you are not sure whether you believe you are called or have the energy to do, tell them: "I can see why you are asking me to do this. I will check both my schedule and the other demands I have, and I will pray over it. *If I can do it*, I will contact you first thing tomorrow, because I don't want to hold you up."

By handling the situation this way, you can have the distance to reflect on what to do. In addition, it eliminates the need to go into a long discussion about why you can't do it if that is your decision.

As committed, compassionate people, we often suffer from "chronic niceness" and go along with requests because we don't want people to feel bad or think poorly of us. But if compassion is to remain full and genuine, and we want to be ready to continue playing our part, then we need to know how to prune. As Henri knew, we must appreciate that psychological pruning is but one piece of the process of *balance*; he had to deal with it constantly himself. For example, in a letter to me on January 13, 1992, Henri wrote: "In answer to your question about how I am doing personally, I simply want to tell you that I am doing quite well, although there are many moments of darkness and of extreme fatigue, but God has been very good to me and given me the energy to continue to respond to many people's needs while keeping me aware of his very great love for me." I valued his honesty.

Taking Nouwen's Words Further:
Presence to Others as a Circle of Grace

Following one of my two meetings with Henri, I reread what is probably his most academic book, *Reaching Out*. This book, which is built on the theme of "availability," points out the importance of balance in life. It reminded me of how Jesus responded when asked a classical rabbinical question: "What is the greatest commandment?" He responded by doing two things a good rabbi would do. First, he put the people at ease, and then he pulled out the psychological rug from under them, to wake them up. He accomplished this by first reaching into Torah for his answers. He selected from both Leviticus and Deuteronomy. First, Jesus selected a "heavy" precept, "You must love God with your whole heart and mind." (As he said this, you can imagine them nodding their heads. What faithful Jewish person would deny this?) Then he reached down and selected a "light" precept from among the 613 laws of the Pharisees of the day, holding it up at the same level as the heavy precept, saying, "And you must love your neighbor as yourself." In emphasizing the neighbor, he was following the murmurings of Exodus and Deuteronomy where the Jews were told that they must not simply find God vertically in prayer but also must find God horizontally in each other.

Jesus said that you must love your neighbor *as yourself.* In doing this, he helped his hearers—and us—recognize the need to discover, share, and enjoy *imago Dei.* Once again, one of the greatest gifts we can share with others is a sense of our own identity, calling, and inner peace. But in order to share this sense, we must have it. And to have it we need to appreciate our ordinariness, learning from the lessons of the desert fathers and mothers who were not swayed or pulled down by the reactions and opinions of others. This ordinariness contains a humility that directs us to center our faith and self-definition in God alone and nothing else. The result: a deep sense of peace in times of turmoil.

The *amma*s and *abba*s modeled a lesson that would come to characterize Franciscan spirituality centuries later: there is nothing so strong as gentleness and nothing so gentle as real strength. Having a better sense of themselves and God enabled the desert fathers and mothers to be compassionate in a freer, more natural, and kinder way. It wasn't that there was never a time for being firm; but their self-knowledge and awareness of their own frailties gave rise to a special sensitivity to individual situations and an appreciation for the value of pacing with respect to spiritual growth of those they were called to guide. A simple desert story illustrates this well.

A few brothers came to see Abba Poemen. They said to him, "Tell us what to do when we see brothers dozing during prayer. Should we pinch them to help them stay awake?" The elder said to them, "Actually what I would do if I saw a brother sleeping is to put his head on my knees and let him rest."[8]

---

8. This is my paraphrase of a saying of the Desert Fathers and Mothers from J.P. Migne, ed. *Patrologia Latina*, Vol. 73 (Paris: Garnier, 1849).

Being compassionate and sensitive to others is not always easy, so we should respect compassionate living as something truly precious. The maturity to have compassion involves accepting and reflecting on our existing deficiencies in this area, and then seeking to correct them. Some things to consider:

- the value of silence and maintaining a true listening stance

- your willingness to risk involvement by forgoing the need for success and praise in every encounter

- appreciating the importance of perseverance, no matter what the apparent odds against you might be

- uncovering your own "surprising points of pain" by seeking to be compassionate and vulnerable

To maintain a listening stance we need to provide silent spaces for people. Then we can think, breathe deeply, experience our own emotions, and better share ourselves with others. Such opportunities are so rare today. English wit, author, and Anglican cleric Sydney Smith once said about a friend, "He has occasional flashes of silence that make his conversation perfectly delightful." To this, I would add the following praise by Irish playwright, poet, and novelist Oscar Wilde for someone he knew who appreciated, as he did, the beauty of silence. Wilde said, "He knew the precise psychological moment to say nothing."

Practicing being present with and for others means recognizing when to be silent and allow others to speak and be heard. In recent years, many of us have become much more aware of how easily our culture becomes inundated by the noise of frequently white, straight, and male-centered voices, with the unfortunate result that sometimes everyone else has trouble being heard. When this happens, everyone loses. But when we are sensitive listeners we can truly be open to different ways of perceiving the world because of differences of experiences, gender, background, and culture, and this expands our awareness of life, others, and God. Otherwise, we are condemned to miss so much in our interactions and to dismiss the beautiful, different ways of understanding and communicating that people who are different from us may manifest. Sensitive listeners become a more compassionate presence and also experience a "circle of grace" by receiving as much as they give.

Freedom from the need for success and praise is also an essential part of a compassionate attitude. It is also a rarity today in all phases of life. Freedom from the need for results means realizing that risk-taking requires an attitude that starts anew each day. It is very much in line with a constant willingness to venture out, even when we really can't see secure results in the future. The result of such an attitude is that life replaces existence. Interaction replaces inaction. And God is experienced both in pleasing and in challenging realities, and never simply thought about on a Sunday morning.

No matter how hot it may be walking along the Tiber River in Rome, or how wet one gets while rushing through the rain on the Strand in London, such actual experiences are always going to be more exhilarating than sitting in one's cool, dry living room at home reading a fancy travel guide. Likewise, people afraid to risk meeting God through compassionate living often use up all their energy dreaming about doing great things or taking important spiritual journeys and then have little energy or courage left to take real steps. People of authentic vision and compassion expend some energy dreaming (we all look at life's spiritual travel guide), but then they have more energy to act. They recognize that discernment isn't simply thinking and then, if possible, acting. Instead, in addition to reflection, discernment requires taking the next step so that God can provide the grace-full invitation to take the one that follows, and the one after that.

This does not mean that reflection isn't valuable or that risking is the same as being rash. Being rash is the result of thoughtless impulse. Risking is knowing there are some things we must do — even when we feel they may involve making mistakes or even failure. The reality we must be willing to look at and accept is that being on the road to finding the truth or seeking improvement is a hazardous process. Still, it is one we cannot avoid if we wish to live a full life, even when the temptation to hold back seems so sensible. We must persevere — and perseverance is a virtue we don't always sufficiently value. We need to recognize the value of an attitude that encourages us not to turn back, even when temporary failure occurs. As the Qur'an states: "Allah is with those who patiently persevere" (2:153).

Having lectured on resilience twice in Cambodia after the Khmer Rouge were pushed into the north of the country, I have been sensitized to stories that reflect the hardiness of the Khmer people as exemplars of the virtue of perseverance. One of those stories was about a number of government pensioners who were handicapped and had their disability payments interminably delayed. Despite their persistent complaints, nothing was done, and they knew that any effort to stage a major protest in the capital city of Phnom Penh might be blocked by the army. As a result, these individuals started at about midnight and joined together to march on the capital. They knew that by starting at that time of day/night, they would be able to get close to the center of the city by dawn, without being stopped by the surprised army. Yet, to do this, the paraplegics and other disabled persons needed to cooperate. And so those in wheelchairs (whose legs had been blown off by landmines) had to be the eyes for the blind pensioners who pushed them along on the dusty roads leading into Phnom Penh.

When you think of this protest being mounted in the dark by these people, you wonder how they could do it. Yet by working together in community, they did. They risked. They persevered. And — yes — they embarrassed the government enough to get their pensions resumed. Too often compassion is not tried or ceases when we focus too much on the odds we are up against instead of being more aware of the holiness of being involved with other people and causes in response to God's call — no matter the outcome. Perseverance is enhanced when we don't lose sight of the importance of responding, rather than being lost in how terrible the situation is.

On another occasion, I worked in Lebanon with caregivers from Aleppo, Syria, who were there to learn how to be more resilient. Often they were being asked to do the impossible by those who came to them for help. I tried to urge them to continue to do what they could, and then allow others and God to take care of the rest. Persistence is a virtue as well as a discipline.

We also need to know our own surprising points of pain when we reach out to others or else we won't be able to stay the course. This is true even for those of us who are professional helpers and healers, mentors, and spiritual directors. For instance, recently I pointed out to a neighbor the generous acts of some people in our community. His dismissive response was, "Oh, they just do it for their own reasons." I was saddened by his bitter response. But I try not to become thrown off by the negative attitudes of some people. Not only do I not want to be impacted by others' darkness, but I also want my psychological arms free to hold the suffering of those who turn to me. There is only so much energy in one person, and I don't want it depleted on those who are marked by narcissism, envy, sarcasm, or other defensive styles. So, in this instance, I was still able to be vulnerable to a person whose perspective was jaded.

In my morning quiet time, my response to such experiences is two-fold: (1) I recognize that I have psychological and spiritual soft spots that I must be more aware of so I don't give away energy that others in true need might require; and (2) I need to heighten my awareness to, and take heart from, people who are doing good in the world — for instance, in our time, by helping out in Ukraine, or settling refugees throughout eastern Europe, and in the U.S. those who are helping all of the Afghans who have recently been forced from their homes and their country. I think of all these people, so I can reinforce my faith in the goodness of humanity.

Here are some questions I ask myself, and that you may wish to consider in your own efforts to embrace compassionate living:

- What are my psychological and spiritual soft spots?

- How can I prevent being unnecessarily dragged down by people's negativity so that I will be able to share the peace that I experience with others?

- Do I realize what a gift a generous attitude is — not only for the recipient but for myself?

Generosity is at the core of a true spiritual attitude. In truly generous behavior there is a profound recognition of the reality emphasized by the Yiddish proverb, "Shrouds are made without pockets." It is so easy to become trapped trapped in the moody, emotional prison of over-preoccupation with self, In other words, so often we worry about ourselves and our own sense of security so much that we actually forget that the best way to be a self-confident and faithful friend of God is to be more sensitive to the needs of others, rather than overly concerned with ourselves. And so we need an appreciation of both the wonder of giving, the death-like vise of greed, and the neurotic concern many of us (including me) have with being taken advantage of by those to whom we give something.

Let's be honest: much of our giving is conditional and really not very wonderful after all. But when we are truly sensitive and do give freely and spontaneously, we set the stage for simple acts of wonder, as described in the following reflection by a young seminarian working in Central America:

Once, at a beach outing, one of the girls who couldn't swim was being tossed about in the rocky edges of the lagoon. I did not hesitate to try to rescue her, in spite of the laughing of the guys when I too ended up being tossed about like a rag doll. Despite the difficulties involved, I somehow persevered and we both managed to get out alive, although I did wind up suffering badly with cuts and bruises.

The real surprise for me, though, was that only later did it occur to me that I myself couldn't swim! And although I spoke little of the incident to others, this whole episode and its implications intrigued me. My sense was I found that the bottom line of the whole encounter was life and its importance.

I think there is something within all of us that makes potential heroes, and that a hero's journey can be a mystical experience. As the theologians Karl Rahner and Meister Eckhart believed, mystical experiences happen every day. I believe that by learning to let go of ourselves, we are placed on the hero's journey to self-discovery, and ultimately the discovery of God within us.[9]

The generosity involved in my friend's sensitivity and action on behalf of the drowning girl set the stage for him to discover more about himself and God. Generosity, when

---

9. I am grateful to Ferdinand Lansang, O.Carm., for sharing this story with me.

it is the source of our attention to others, produces good re-sults for all involved — even though we may not clearly see them at the time.

Henri Nouwen gave a great deal of attention to gen-erosity and friendship because he valued community, even though he struggled living at times — as we all do — within communities, and he also lived alone during much of his life as a professor. But, after joining L'Arche, Henri recog-nized again the emptiness he felt without other people sur-rounding him.

When we live with others and truly accompany them, we are often exposed to their troubles and pain. The walk in darkness with others is never easy, but the message Jesus left in scripture is that our compassionate presence to others is worth all the love we can put in it. St. Paul wrote: "Blessed be the God and Father of our Lord Jesus Christ, the Father of mercies and God of all consolation, who consoles us in all our affliction, so that we may be able to console those who are in any affliction with the consolation with which we ourselves are consoled by God" (2 Cor 1:3-4). I think we sense that this is true no matter what happens. And we are convinced of it when we are allowed to see and hear some of the workings of God that have come about during our encounters with others.

There was a time when a person, looking back on time together with me, wrote this note: "And what will I leave behind from our relationship? I will leave my 'stuckness,' my unconsciousness, my shame and guilt, my repressed pain, resentment, and depression.... And what will I take with me, what has been awakened through the gift of our relationship? My playfulness, my love of life, my sense of

wonder, my gratitude, my openness, and my wholeness."
In reading her words, I too was grateful. I had been her
mentor. I was grateful for her wonderful presence in the
world and thankful to God that together we could better
welcome the bright little child she had been before abuse
had crushed her initial energetic presence in the world.
What better can we do for each other than this? Nouwen's
letters are full of similar affirmations from those with
whom he walked side by side.

Reflecting further on that relationship of mine, I was
happy that we could see the talented adult she had
begun to embrace during the past few years of our time
together. The joy we could both feel now was that the
abuse of long ago, which we had discussed and "worked
through," would not be the last word in the formation of
her identity. To the contrary, it became the first word in a
new life for her that positively impacted those she met.
Deo gratias!

I also recognized that in meeting with this person (and
others with whom I walked in a mentoring or therapeutic
relationship), a sensitive understanding of the uniqueness
of myself—both my sins and my talents—had helped me
recognize and appreciate better what I needed to say and
do. Knowledge of my gifts as well as my limitations enabled me to be a better healing presence than I would have
been otherwise. I could both fathom joy and weather personal darkness, and this helped me encounter others in
their uniqueness.

Nouwen counseled thousands of people with his
books. That is, in fact, the power of the written word. In his
books and in his letters Nouwen's compassion and humility shone through. For example, in a letter from the early
1980s, responding to a woman whom he had never met, he

offered her many suggestions and then concluded by saying: "I just hope that these few thoughts at least will point in a direction that might be helpful to you. If not, please let me know and we will try other ways."[10]

Theologian Sallie McFague, in *Models of God*, recognizes both the gift and challenges of true friendship in her chapter, "God as Friend."[11] She points out several qualities of friendship that are important to all of us as we consider the theme of compassion. The first is that friendship is based on parity. A friend who is neither constantly coming to our rescue nor victimizing is someone to be valued. Interdependence is a value that gives in different ways, at different times to *both* people. This is what I mean when I speak of creating, and living in, a "circle of grace."

Friendship must also be open so that both parties experience a sense of freedom, rather than a sense of imprisonment. An extreme of the dangers involved when such freedom is absent is experienced especially by those who have been physically, sexually, or spiritually abused.

There is also an inclusive element in friendship (as well as a welcoming of diversity in community) that leads to growth—because real friends welcome change rather than worship the status quo. This must be expressed in action, not just in words. For instance, many women and people of color have said to me that they are told they are equal and that people are sensitive to their needs and appreciative of the gift of their teachings and heritage, but these things are not really true.

---

10. *Love, Henri: Letters on the Spiritual Life*, ed. Gabrielle Earnshaw (New York: Convergent Books, 2018), 84.

11. Sallie McFague, *Models of God* (Philadelphia: Fortress Press, 1987), chapter 6: "God as Friend."

Furthermore, we need to recognize that all people are different from one another—especially when they are in emotional, physical, or spiritual pain. We can even see this clearly in animals. For example, when a cat is sick, it often walks away, hides, and wants to be left alone. On the other hand, what do dogs do when they are sick? They are usually dramatic actors who lie underfoot in the middle of the kitchen floor looking up as if to say: Do something! Can't you see that I am sick?[12] Similar differences can be seen with people, and this fact must be recognized to achieve healing results whether they be physical, psychological, or spiritual.

If a physician treats everyone who comes into her consultation room complaining of belly pain as if they needed a splenectomy, she will achieve uneven surgical results, to put it mildly. If psychologists, counselors, or clinical social workers don't have a broad enough theory of personality to allow for many individual differences, they will erroneously and simplistically treat everyone alike—or worse, as if the person were like them. In the few cases where this actually happens, there might be some measure of success, but in most instances a patient or client receiving such unimaginative, uniform treatment is headed for personal disaster.

As in counseling or medicine, this can happen too in life in general. We need to be sensitive to the spiritual wonders and talents of each person we meet. We need to begin to appreciate others for their wonderful though

---

12. I am grateful to my friend, Jeff Dauses, for this funny little insight.

sometimes hidden uniqueness. As another Yiddish proverb goes: "If all pulled in one direction, the world would keel over." Once we recognize this, our views of, and interactions with, others can become richer and less filled with stress, disappointment, and judgment. We are called and challenged to be compassionate — to recognize and reflect the spiritual gifts of others so that they can then own and build upon them, rather than let them lie fallow or atrophy.

As Nouwen counseled in a letter to a friend who was feeling uncertain about herself and her ministry, "Somewhere you have to hear again very clearly the blessing of God that says, 'You are my beloved daughter; on you my favor rests.'"[13] We all need to hear this, to know this.

Yet, to do this and to continually enrich our ability to be a beneficent and healthy presence to others, we must become a true friend to ourselves and, just as importantly, feel the freedom and love to be vulnerable with God in prayer.

Mentoring Moments...

(Quotes from Henri Nouwen to provide an opening for you to reflect on the theme of compassion and community)

"A real friend is someone who doesn't walk off when there are no solutions or answers, but sticks by you and remains faithful to you. It often turns

---

13. *Love, Henri*, 257.

out that the one who gives us the most comfort is not the person who says, 'Do this, say that, go there'; but the one, even if there is no good advice to give, says, 'Whatever happens, I'm your friend; you can count on me.' The older you become the more you discover that your joy and happiness depend on such friendships. The great secret in life is that suffering, which often seems to be unbearable, can become, through compassion, a source of new life and new hope."

(*Letters to Marc about Jesus*)[14]

"We can take a lot of physical and even mental pain when we know that it truly makes us part of the life we live together in the world. But when we feel cut off from the human family, we quickly lose heart."

(*Making All Things New*, 33)

"Let us not fool ourselves by thinking that spiritual formation can be possible in a highly privatized milieu. It might in fact have the opposite effect. When word, silence, and guidance as ways to the heart are introduced into a basically individualistic milieu they might simply feed our narcissistic tendencies and lead to a spiritual self-centeredness. Then so-called 'spiritual formation' leads to small heartedness and moves us away from the biblical call to be shepherds of the people of God. It is therefore quite understandable that

---

14. Henri J. M. Nouwen, *Letters to Marc about Jesus: Living a Spiritual Life in a Material World* (New York: HarperOne, 2009), 33.

wherever authentic spiritual growth takes place there is always a strengthening of community and that wherever authentic community is found there always is a growing desire for a deepening of the spiritual life."

("What Do You Know by Heart? Learning Spirituality")[15]

---

15. Henri J. M. Nouwen, "What Do You Know by Heart? Learning Spirituality," *Sojourners* 6, no. 8 (August 1977): 14.

Vulnerability and Prayer

The way of simple prayer, when we are faithful to it and practice it at regular times, slowly leads us to an experience of rest and opens us to God's active presence. Moreover, we can take this prayer with us into a very busy day. When, for instance, we have spent twenty minutes in the early morning sitting in the presence of God with the words "The Lord is my Shepherd," they may slowly build a little nest for themselves in our heart and stay there for the rest of our busy day.

—Henri Nouwen[1]

We listen to lectures affirming the importance of prayer, but we really think that our people need actions and not prayer and that praying is good when you really have nothing else to do. I wonder if under the surface of our religiosity we do not have

---

1. Henri J. M. Nouwen, *The Way of the Heart: Connecting with God through Prayer, Wisdom, and Silence* (New York: Ballantine, 2003), 83.

great doubts about God's effectiveness in our world, about his interest in us — yes, even about his presence among us.... When we speak of our age as a secular age, we must first of all be willing to become aware of how deeply this secularism has entered into our own hearts and how doubt, hesitation, suspicion, anger, and even hatred corrode our relationship with God.

—Henri Nouwen[2]

Once, when Henri visited Mother Teresa, he asked her what he should do to be a good priest. So, when I visited him once, I thought I would ask something similar.

I said, "Henri, I have described for you the work I do as someone who works almost exclusively with helping and healing professionals such as priests, women and men religious (sisters and brothers), educators, physicians, nurses, social workers, psychologists, counselors, chaplains and psychiatrists. Is there something that I should do to support and center me in this role?"

He gave me an incredulous, almost impatient, look. Then, waving his hand in the air (he often did this), he said, "Well, that is such a big question."

I waited, giving him the look I imagine Jacob must have given the angel as he struggled with him all night waiting for an answer. My look also conveyed what the disciples of the desert *abba*s and *amma*s did when they demanded a "word" from those they respected as sages. I can wait. I *will* wait.

---

2. *Clowning in Rome: Reflections on Solitude, Celibacy, Prayer, and Contemplation* (New York: Image Books, 2000), 26.

Finally, when he could see that I was not about to leave until I had a response of some sort, in an almost exasperated voice Henri finally said: "Take about twenty minutes each morning in silence and solitude and put yourself in the presence of the Lord. If you wish, read a bit of scripture before you do this. Then, all will be well."

Simple words. Ones that I have tried to follow my whole life since, and would suggest others do as well. Knowing people's different types of resistance to spending time in silence and solitude, I often suggest they start with only two minutes. When I get a reaction that such a period seems too short, I respond, "Well, how often and how long are you doing it now? Regularity is more important than length. Hopefully, once the practice is set in place, you will then extend the period and also want to put yourself in the presence of the Lord at different times in your day as well."

In his writings, Henri would describe such morning periods as a chance to place in his day and his life a "nest" upon which to rest and to which he could return. Although it sounds simple, and it can be, it is not easy for most of us. It hasn't been easy for me. It also wasn't simple for Henri, but hope was always a part of his sense of vulnerability as well. In *The Return of the Prodigal Son* he wrote:

> For most of my life I have struggled to find God, to know God, to love God. I have tried hard to follow the guidelines of the spiritual life—pray always, work for others, read the Scriptures—and to avoid the many temptations to dissipate myself. I have failed many times but always tried again, even when I was close to despair....Now I wonder whether I have sufficiently realized that during all

this time God has been trying to find me, know me, and love me.[3]

Vulnerability is one of the rare traits of a true mentor of prayer and life. Henri modeled this trait in every way. It was one of the features of his books that reduced the resistance of his readers to what he had to say. In *Life of the Beloved*, he wrote: "There are many things I would like to say to you about our brokenness. But where to begin? Perhaps the simplest beginning would be to say that our brokenness reveals something about who we are. Our sufferings and pains are not simply bothersome interruptions of our lives; rather, they touch us in our uniqueness and our most intimate individuality. The way I am broken tells you something unique about me. The way you are broken tells me something unique about you."[4]

It was also evident to everyone who knew him personally. Nouwen was able to share his own frailties in a way that had all of us become willing in new ways to look at our own. In fact, he was often torn between wanting to help others and being so overwhelmed personally that he knew somehow he must set some boundaries, take a breath — and pray.

In a letter to me on December 27, 1987, Henri wrote, "I really want to be of as much help to you as possible, but this is a very hard time for me and I find myself under much emotional stress, so I really need to take some distance and

---

3. Henri J. M. Nouwen, *The Return of the Prodigal Son: A Story of Homecoming* (New York: Image Books, 1994), 110.

4. Henri J. M. Nouwen, *Life of the Beloved: Spiritual Living in a Secular World* (New York: Crossroad, 2002), 87.

to create some new inner space where I can really hear the voice of God's love. Please keep me in your prayers. Thanks so much for your friendship and support."

The following spring, in a letter of May 19, 1988, he shared with me: "What I am experiencing is a really deep spiritual crisis in which I realize that God wants all of my heart, not simply a part of it. It seems as if He wants to test my faithfulness and my commitment in a new way. He is really asking me to let go of everything that does not bring me closer to Him. He calls me to a more generous prayer life and to a more fearless ministry. This year is a kind of desert year to purify my heart. It is painful, but also full of grace."

Almost one year after that, on March 23, 1989, he wrote of his appreciation for my support: "Thank you for your kind note in response to my accident. Although in the beginning I was seriously ill and close to death, I am now healing quickly and getting my health back. The whole incident was a real blessing, and I feel much closer to God, and to all the people around me. Thanks for your care and attention."

Nouwen was honest about his challenges and this endeared him to me — and, I know, to many others. In June 18, 1990, he wrote, "Your challenge to live more at peace without having to be right in front of death is really an important one, and I hear that challenge and want to be very attentive to the questions you raise."

As can be seen in all of these letters, Henri, in addition to his health challenges and other frailties, was beginning to see even more clearly after what he described as the most emotionally trying time in his life — from October 1987 until June 1988. During this period, he was able to express his personal anguish to his counselors. Years later, he expressed this to his readers through his book, *The Inner*

Voice of Love. We all came to understand better his encounters with darkness, rejection, and eventually embracing the light of God.

Most of us don't have personalities like Henri's — so creative, so pliable, so Spirit-led — but what he communicated in this book are lessons all of us can benefit from. They are the lessons of a "wounded healer," not someone who is totally accomplished, like some religious people claim to be today.

Henri felt inexhaustible needs, a sense of abandonment, and exposure to ridicule by others as never before during this particularly vulnerable time. He knew that he needed not only psychotherapy but also a chance to close off the world so that he could be with people who truly cared for him. He needed also a new and deeper presence to God that required letting go of previously understood images of the Divine.

He revisited a reality he had shared in *The Genesee Diary* that had continued to plague him: namely, no one person can satisfy all your needs. As a result, you need to honor the value of community, and you have to respect the boundaries of others, so you don't ask or seek to offer what can only be given by God. In seeing all of this more clearly, he began to recognize that all people, especially caring people, will experience inner emptiness and pain that you or others cannot take away. In Henri's words, "It exists far deeper than you can reach."[5]

He would also share in *The Inner Voice of Love* that a "deeply satisfying friendship became the road to my

---

5. Henri J. M. Nouwen, *The Inner Voice of Love: A Journey through Anguish to Freedom* (New York: Image Books, 1999), 55.

anguish, because soon I discovered that the enormous space that had been opened for me could not be filled by the one who opened it. I became possessive, needy, and dependent, and when the friendship finally had to be interrupted, I fell apart. I felt abandoned, rejected, and betrayed. Indeed, the extremes touched each other."[6] He shared all of this about eight years after it happened because he felt it would be a source of consolation to see how "light and darkness, hope and despair, love and fear, are never very far from each other, and that spiritual freedom often requires a fierce spiritual battle."[7]

From a psychological vantage point, he was mentoring us in understanding spiritual suffering, and from a psychologist's perspective, he was showing us how to experience what is now referred to as "posttraumatic growth." Henri was teaching us that inner pain can be converted into deeper inner peace, freedom, and even joy, when it is attended to with gentleness and clarity, personally and with others, and cognitively—most of all, with God in prayer. Yet, for this to happen we must recognize, surface, and welcome our resistances to embracing the truth and love in ways that will move us out of our comfortable place. We must do this if we are to experience feelings of peace, freedom, and joy.

Knowing this, in *A Cry for Mercy*—a book we haven't yet mentioned, which includes beautiful prayers composed during a return visit to the Trappist Abbey of the Genesee—Nouwen then offers the following prayer to God: "I know how great my resistance is, how quickly I choose darkness instead of the light. But I also know that

---

6. Nouwen, *The Inner Voice of Love*, xv.

7. Nouwen, *The Inner Voice of Love*, xviii, xix.

you keep calling me into the light, where I can see not only my sins but your gracious face as well."[8] He follows this up with a plea that he remain open to God's initiatives in his life. And then, on an even more basic level, he confesses his inability to pray as he would desire.

Taking Nouwen's Words Further: Facing Our Resistances to Prayer

Henri was very aware of the impact memories have on our lives. In his recorded message, "The Christ-Memory in Our Lives" (published in the 1990s as an audio cassette) and his book, *The Living Reminder*, he addressed the question, "What does it mean to be a living memory of Jesus Christ?" He recognized that memories can play various roles. They can be healing and sustaining, as well as guides for future actions. The *way* we remember them, he rightly appreciates, is more important than the actual events themselves. He puts it this way:

> The older we grow the more we have to remember, and at some point we realize that most, if not all, of what we have is memory. Our memory plays a central role in our sense of being. Our pains and joys, our feelings of grief and satisfaction, are not simply dependent on the events of our lives, but also, and even more so, on the ways we remember these events. The events of our lives are probably less important than the form they take in the totality of

---

8. Henry J. M. Nouwen, *A Cry for Mercy: Prayers from the Genesee* (New York: Image Books, 2002), 24–25.

our story. Different people remember a similar ill-
ness, accident, success, or surprise in very different
ways, and much of their sense of self derives less
form what happened than from how they remember what happened, how they have placed the past
events into their own personal history.[9]

In my own clinical practice, this point of Henri's has
been borne out again and again. In one case, you will have
someone who has been abused early in life and this trauma
leads them to be more compassionate toward others. Another person with much less tragic beginnings is able only
to just stay afloat for the rest of her life. While still another
feels that life owes him, and he drains his children and wife
of all vitality because he has been so hurt. This often results
in children trying to compensate for their parents' neediness and inability to consider the concerns of others by constantly making excuses for their behavior. Survivors of
horrible tragedies early in life have often demonstrated
that—because they could not receive what they needed
early on—they developed symptoms and signs of what is
referred to today as borderline or narcissistic personality.
They sometimes came to see life only in terms of what
needs they had and how they demanded these needs be
met because of what they had gone through themselves. We
are learning more all the time about how we carry trauma
around with us, and even how we pass it on in our genes.

Henri noted that—for all of us—our most profound
emotions are tied to memories, and to the questions and

---

9. Henry J. M. Nouwen, *The Living Reminder: Service and Prayer in
Memory of Jesus Christ* (New York: HarperOne, 2009), 19.

comments these memories raise in our minds at the end of a day. For example:

- We experience remorse... "Why did I say that?"

- We experience shame... "What will people think of me?"

- We experience guilt... "Have I hurt or offended someone?"

- We experience pride... "Look at all the trophies (children, etc...) I have. "

- We experience gratitude... "It was a privilege to make a contribution."

Nouwen appreciated that people are also wounded by memories. I have seen that his words are correct. Past sad moments and previous regretted turns do impact many of us. Most people tend to be very hard on themselves. This is especially — and maybe surprisingly — so for those who have dedicated themselves to a life of compassion. When teachers, physicians, nurses, ministers, and even mental health professionals look back, they often forget to temper clarity with kindness and humility.

Sitting with different types of caregivers, as I have throughout my professional life, at about the tenth session much of their inner darkness is shared. And as I listen to their sense of personal failure, professional mistakes, feelings of being misunderstood and unappreciated, I can see and hear the hurt in their lives. Nouwen often did this kind of work with others, and he lived this kind of pain himself.

He once wrote in *The Living Reminder*, "It is no exaggeration to say that the suffering we most frequently encounter in the ministry is a suffering of memories. They are the wounding memories that ask for healing. Feelings of alienation, loneliness, separation; feelings of anxiety, fear, suspicion; and related symptoms such as nervousness, sleeplessness, nail-biting [which Nouwen himself did]—these all are part of the forms which certain memories have taken. These memories wound because they are often deeply hidden in the center of our being and very hard to reach." To this he then adds, "It is from this hidden place that they escape healing and cause so much harm....Forgetting the past is like turning our most intimate teacher against us."[10]

I must confess that even though I have learned the dangers of being overly empathic, I have sometimes gone to bed at night feeling intensely with the quiet despair of those I have counseled. In addition, their suffering does sometimes serve as a mirror, and at times it makes me recall my own past sad moments and some of the previous turns in life that I regret because, like everyone else, I have failed, too—and failed miserably. (Given my outgoing personality, when I fail—I fail big time!)

But as I reflect on my patients and their sorrows, I also think: *If only they could see how good they are.* If only they could also appreciate the positive difference they have made in so many people's lives. If only they could look back with the understanding that the more they are involved, statistically the more they are going to fail. If only they could more deeply appreciate that each style of inter-

---

10. Nouwen, *The Living Reminder*, 20, 21, 22.

acting with others is a gift—and a cross at times. And when I turn those wishes back onto myself, I smile and fall asleep knowing that I will not give up being compassionate because I am not perfect. Instead, maybe the knowledge of my own personal and professional past shortcomings will make me even more of an understanding, helpful, and caring person because I also periodically travel in the same dark forest that they do—and still have hope. This was the case for Henri when he said he looked at his own "small life" and felt in important ways it was connected to Christ's.

We see this reflected in *The Living Reminder*, where he writes: "To be a living memory of Jesus Christ, therefore, means to reveal the connections between our small sufferings and the great story of God's suffering in Jesus Christ, between our little life and the great life of God with us. By lifting our painful forgotten memories out of the egocentric, individualistic, private sphere, Jesus Christ heals our pains."[11] Nouwen sees the challenge Christians face in recognizing that when they experience suffering, they often do so in ways that reflect a disconnectedness from God. We are no longer walking in the presence of God, we are not mindful of both the source of our life and where we are headed. And so, he recognizes that when this happens, "we start walking in a vicious circle, and pulling others into it."[12]

Life can be very difficult, and even harsh. People who live a truly prayerful life know this and don't avoid the dark realities. Instead, they bring these realities to God at

---

11. Nouwen, *The Living Reminder*, 25.

12. Nouwen, *The Living Reminder*, 29.

liturgy or in community prayer, during periods of solitude, and in reflective moments of prayerfulness during the activity of the day.

Our joy does not come from a triumphant God who keeps us above the fray, a sullen God who says suffering is all we can expect, or a private God we hide away with from the world (although it is natural to want a God like these at times). The joy and peace of a life of prayer is in welcoming and being sensitive to a truthful and faithful God who will call, teach, save, and love us — no matter how harsh life becomes for us and others.

To have a deep sensitivity to God is to follow a calling to live in the classic tension of welcoming God into our lives both in transformative private and communal prayer and during times of encounter with others during the activity of the day. To avoid either side of the tension is to court either the disaster of quietism (a prayer life that is unreal and indulgent) or an undisciplined activism which will eventually only lead to withdrawal and discouragement. A deep sensitivity to God must be the source of our sensitivity to ourselves, others, and the world around us. And so, we need to learn to embrace the classic tension between prayer and action.

Waking up in Thailand one day, I rose to the sound of my alarm, quickly got dressed, had several cups of strong tea, and walked over to a nearby beach with a new friend from the retreat center. We went to take a swim and pray at sunrise in what was once known as the Gulf of Siam.

In some ways it was perfect — spiritually uplifting! The sun was about to rise on the calm sea, and as I floated in the warm water I noticed young Buddhist monks walking along the shore with full begging bowls, having successfully made their rounds to request food from respectful

Thais who wished to support their quest and gain merit. But as I continued to float I could also see the construction of mammoth new buildings on the beach and the morning outlines of existing hotels that I had recently learned were pouring raw sewage directly into the Gulf. In fact, I had been warned that I was taking a chance by swimming in what had once been a pristine but was now a quite polluted body of water. I also knew that as the day advanced, the monks who were now walking along in silence would be replaced by European, Japanese, and American male tourists and the women they had hired to be their sexual companions. A scene of sexual degradation of women would be the afternoon's reality replacing that of respect and holiness now visible at the shore. The monks' saffron robes were a symbol of hope, but new images that spoke of loneliness, competition, greed, hostility, and abuse of power would follow. With that thought, I recognized that if society continues to move in these destructive directions, any spirituality that would be true and real would have to take stock of such contradictions. I couldn't simply have my morning prayer and serenity and ignore all the rest.

This leaves us with the classic tension between prayer and action that Nouwen knew well and referred to during his brief stay in South America. On the one hand, he knew we needed a hope based on a deep faith nurtured in silent prayer; and, on the other hand, he also knew that ours should be a proven faith anchored and developed in encounters with each other. To forsake one end of the spectrum is to endanger the other. To avoid silence and solitude is to court burnout and disillusionment. Yet, to foster quietism while forests are devastated and people are being abused because of their gender, race, ethnic, or financial state, is to let our time of spiritual solitude become like beautiful-looking but stagnant water. It may be calm and still, but it will also be putrid, not the life-giving water of God.

Real spirituality—life-giving for us and for others—dawns only when God is as real as the problems and joys we face each day, which is impossible if we cut our prayers off from our responsibilities, daily realities, and truer and more complete appreciation of who we are as believers and human beings. We need to let the memories we have, memories that can teach us, do just that; if they lie dormant, we will be diminished and we will allow ourselves to quietly submit to secularism, possibly under a shroud of religious words.

The world can be a desperate place for so many. I see it in the faces of the abused and neglected as well as those who care for them when they come in for therapy or spiritual mentoring. And I encounter it on a daily basis in the broader arena of today's news reports on wars and new dictatorships. Hope sustains us.

I recall a news story in the aftermath of the Bosnian War when a member of a relief service was walking through a bombed-out city and encountered a man trimming flowers and bushes around the rubble of what used to be his home. When asked what he was doing, the man simply replied that his wife and daughters had died in the building and he came each day to tend to their grave so it would be beautiful. How can we, like this man, continue to be sensitive and have hope when faced with terrible situations? How can our faith stand against continuing atrocities and despair? While it is no less painful for spiritually alive persons than for others to do this, unlike others, we have no choice. Our faith calls us to an attitude of firm hope.

That hope must be based to a great degree on concrete encounters with God in silence and solitude. Otherwise, the despair that is sold on news websites, television, and in our social media feeds every morning will surely win out. It is only when we are reminded of the duplicity in our own hearts that we avoid the dangers of harshly criticizing others as charlatans. It is only when we see our response to pain as being part of God's overall response that we can see in our aloneness with God that we are never really alone.

None of this is new, of course, but the need for generosity — in how we embrace God's gifts to us in contemplation and action — may be needed now more than ever before. If we are honest, this presents us with a problem. Once again, being a healing and compassionate presence to others sounds wonderful in the abstract, but when we are faced with misery, pain, and others' agendas (as well as our own), there is a temptation to pull back and sit, rationalizing that it is enough to take care of our own needs rather than cross boundaries and do harm to ourselves in trying to meet the sometimes impossible demands of others. And so, prayer is not a nicety but a necessity if we are to have the purest intentions possible.

To conclude near where we started, like the desert fathers and mothers of the fourth and fifth centuries, to pray now is to meet resistances with faith, hope, and compassion during our times in silence and solitude. The desert taught us and prepared us to return to the world. We can see spiritual and psychological obstacles to contemplation operating when we say we are too busy to pray. Nouwen taught me this again and again. Although we may have a very full daily schedule, we can always find time for what we value. Therefore, if we say we treasure prayer, then our actions must prove it. And for this to happen, we need to recognize and resolve the following resistances to time alone with God:

- lack of familiarity

- boredom

- avoidance of shame

- failure to see results

- inappropriate use of sacred scripture

- fear

- inability to see the role of love

That first resistance, a lack of familiarity with prayer (we don't pray often because we don't feel "at home" doing it) is self-perpetuating. It is also a false problem. It isn't real. We overcome the problem by moving past it, essentially treating it as if it doesn't exist. To illustrate the point, Nouwen explains his own process:

> I had the fantasy that one day God just might break through the hard shell of my resistance and reveal himself to me in such an intensive and convincing way that I would be able to let my "idols" go and commit myself unreservedly to him. John Eudes was not too surprised by the fantasy and said, "You want God to appear to you in the way your passions desire, but these passions make you blind to his presence now. Focus on the nonpassionate part of yourself and realize God's presence there. Let that part grow in you and make your decision from

there. You will be surprised to see how powers that seem invincible shrivel away."[13]

The unfamiliar must become our friend in prayer, the unspoken must offer God's words, and the vague become a place for something new in our hearts to be formed, something that can be lived out in concrete ways with others.

Then comes boredom, another issue in quiet prayer. This happens because often the problem is that our prayer is too artificial, bland, and compartmentalized. If our prayer is dull, we must then ask ourselves, *When was the last time I spoke with God about things that really mattered to me in my daily life?* Do we share our angers, joys, impulses, secrets, addictions, and anxieties? Do we talk to the Lord about our perversions, desires, needs, resistances, and failures? For instance, when did we last say to God: "I love you," "Down deep, I doubt you exist," or "I hate the way you are running this world!"

In line with the resistance of boredom is the next potential obstacle to prayer: not wanting to challenge our shame. Kahlil Gibran wrote in one of his lesser known works, "Should we all confess our sins to one another we would all laugh at one another for our lack of originality."[14] Even though this is so, we resist looking at our sins and failings because we believe they prove that we are people who should not be appreciated and loved.

Failure to see results is another common resistance to taking out time in prayer. There is a Zen saying that ad-

---

13. Henri J. M. Nouwen, *The Genesee Diary: Report from a Trappist Monastery* (New York: Image Books, 1981), 71.

14. Kahlil Gibran, *Sand and Foam* (New York: Knopf, 1966), 45.

vises, "Face reality and unwilled change will take place." In prayer, as we stand naked before God, there is a movement in our unconscious attitude that we may not notice, a movement that results in our relating to ourselves and others in a freer way. It is a basic and beautiful fruit of true prayer. The psychological reason for this is that when our attitude is healthy, our actions will naturally be good without our even having to think about them.

Likewise, prayer produces changes that we may not see directly in our environment but which make all the difference in life. One bishop shared with his priests and the people of his diocese that he really didn't know whether the prayers he was saying made any difference, but he did know one thing: when he stopped praying, many good things seemed to stop as well. This is a point worth keeping in mind, since society trains us to look for results in certain specific ways. This can lead to discouragement when we don't see things happen at the time and in the way we want.

An inappropriate or inadequate use of scripture also can result in our feeling lost because our God is too vague and our understanding of the history of relationships between God and the human person is either almost absent or too intellectual. Unfortunately, religious people are sometimes the worst with respect to reading scripture because it is not new for them. They know how all the stories end! Yet, sacred scripture—especially when read prior to a period of a time in silence and solitude—must be more personally challenging than this.

Once a young man approached the famous Rabbi Israel ben Eliezer (known as the "Baal Shem Tov," the founder of Hasidic Judaism) and asked how he might become a rabbi. The rabbi sent him away with the advice that he seriously read Torah. In several months, the young man was back again, saying with more confidence, "Rebbe, I have been through Torah ten times!" To which the Baal Shem Tov responded quietly and gently, "Yes son, but how many times has Torah been through you?" For those of us confident in our knowledge of scripture, such that we mostly ignore it, we can learn from this. A Christian teacher, the theologian Karl Barth, used to challenge his students, "When reading scripture and you ask, 'What is this book saying?' it should respond, 'Who is this that is asking?' Our identity should be on the line."

Another resistance is fear of spending time in silence and solitude with God. This is real for many people. There is a Cameroonian proverb that says, "He who asks the questions cannot avoid the answers." Those who have encountered God in prayer have discovered this in surprising ways — and as we read the spiritual classics or the comments of modern prophetic religious figures whom we admire, we see and hear it in their words.

Two of my favorite of the more classic modern and well-known statements that reflect the fear that is a natural part of encounter with the living God are from Paul Tillich and Metropolitan Anthony of Sourozh (Andrei Borisovich Bloom). It is Paul Tillich who said, "If you have never run away from your God, I wonder who your God is?" And Metropolitan Anthony echoed these sentiments in suggesting that to meet God is like entering the cave of a tiger. He said, "The realm of God is dangerous [to our preconditioned notions]. You must enter into it and not just seek information about it."[15]

---

15. Anthony Bloom, *Beginning to Pray* (New York: Paulist Press, 1970), 15.

True prayer encourages us to let go. In prayer we fear risking the presence of the Spirit in our lives in a way that ends in our not being able to control God's presence, message, or image. We say we want the love of the relationship, but we often unconsciously finish the sentence with "in our way and on our terms." Once again, there is no bargaining with freedom. Either the relationship is real and open or it isn't. And if it isn't, then prayer suffers accordingly.

In true prayer, our idols come to light and we see how we really prefer the darkness where we don't have to face them. We begin to see a glimmer of our denials and avoidances; we begin to recognize the buds of spiritual self-awareness which we can pray over and share with others and this is of course good. We can then with true attention ask, "Who is my God?" and do so while recognizing Jesus' statement, "Where your treasure is, there your heart will be also" (Mt 6:21). And so we can begin to see where all our mental energy goes, and that is what will tell us what we truly hold as divine.

Finally, a core resistance to prayer is the inability to see the role of love. Gertrud Mueller Nelson in her book, *Here All Dwell Free,* wrote:

> Romantic love is not an aberration, it is heady stuff that launches ships and makes the world go round. It is a powerful taste of the divine as we experience it in one another. It is also the necessary vision that allows one to be crazy and daring enough to make a commitment.[16]

---

16. Gertrud Mueller Nelson, *Here All Dwell Free: Stories to Heal the Wounded Feminine* (New York: Paulist Press, 1999), 62.

The irony is that even though prayer is by its very definition an act of love and a recognition of being loved, sometimes love is not as present as it should be. The result is that prayer becomes a dutiful act, or the enactment of techniques.

Many of us at one time or other think that we can gain heaven or pray properly with our own wills and by our own efforts. We fail to recognize that while discipline and methods of prayer may be helpful, prayer is first and foremost a relationship based on love: God's and ours.

Contemplation is also first and foremost a gift. It involves both the freedom of God and our own initiatives. When we pray, one of the first questions we need to ask ourselves is about the attitude with which we are entering the relationship with God. If it is with the respect, humility, and awe that are part of our love of the Divine and made more concrete by an embrace of sacred scripture, then we are coming to the encounter with a proper sense of the depth. But if it is just with a sense of obligation, a feeling that we ought to be there, then the result will be one of frustration and, as Henri pointed out, we are then involved in what turns out to be essentially a game of hide-and-seek with a God whom we are not even sure is interested in us; the image of God hanging on the cross is absent, along with his extreme love for us.

Obviously, there are resistances to prayer just as to true compassion. But simple faithfulness to prayer and action — though not easy, spectacular, or seemingly revolutionary enough to our minds — will bring with it a deep sensitivity to our presence to others, those whom we encounter, and God. In all of these areas, Nouwen's encounter with, and sharing of, his insights into desert wisdom, ordinariness, compassion, vulnerability and prayer are like the spiritual and psychological headlights on a car. They offer us enough light to discern the next step—to learn how to mentor ourselves and to learn from the wisdom others have shared.

Mentoring Moments...

(Quotes from Henri Nouwen to provide an opening for you to reflect on the theme of vulnerability and prayer)

"Why, O Lord, is it so hard for me to keep my heart directed toward you? Why do the many little things I want to do, and the many people I know, keep crowding my mind, even during the hours when I am totally free to be with you and you alone? Why does my mind wander off in so many directions, and why does my heart desire the things that lead me astray? Are you not enough for me? Do I keep doubting your love and care, your mercy and grace? Do I keep wondering, in the center of my being, whether you will give me all I need if I just keep my eyes on you?...The only thing you ask of me is not to hide from you, not to run away in despair, not to act as if you were a relentless despot."

(A Cry for Mercy, 26–27)

"If I were to let my life be taken over by what is urgent, I might very well never get around to what is essential. It's so easy to spend your whole time being preoccupied with urgent matters and never starting to live, really to live....It is possible to lead a very wholesome, emotionally rich, and 'sensible' life without being a spiritual person: that is, without knowledge or personal experience of the terrain where the meaning and goal of our human existence are hidden."

(Letters to Marc about Jesus, 3, 5)

"Jesus responds [to the condition of feeling fragmented and worried], being filled yet unfulfilled, very busy yet never at home. He wants to bring us to the place where we belong. But his call to live a spiritual life can only be heard when we are willing honestly to confess our own homeless and worrying existence and recognize its fragmenting effect on our daily life. Only then can a desire for our true home develop. It is of this desire that Jesus speaks when he says, 'Do not worry.... Set your hearts on his kingdom first...and all these other things will be given you as well.'"

(Making All Things New, 37)

"We want to forget the pains of the past—our personal, communal, and national traumas—and live as if they did not really happen. But by not remembering them we allow the forgotten memories to become independent forces that can exert a crippling effect on our functioning as human beings. When this happens, we become strangers to ourselves because we cut down our own history to a pleasant, comfortable size and try to make it conform to our daydreams.... When Jesus says, 'It is not the healthy who need the doctor but the sick' (Mark 2:17), he affirms that only those who face their wounded condition can be available for healing and so enter into a new way of living."

(The Living Reminder, 21–22)

III

SPIRITUAL MENTORING

WITH HENRI NOUWEN

Mentoring Yourself
and Guiding Others

You will teach them to fly, but they will not fly your flight. You will teach them to dream, but they will not dream your dream. You will teach them to live, but they will not live your life. Nevertheless, in every flight, in every life, in every dream, the print of the way you taught them will remain.
— Attributed to St. Teresa of Calcutta

Henri Nouwen emerged as a superb Christian teacher who will surely stand the test of time.
— Richard Rohr[1]

Mentoring is a grace and an art which even the most impressive of individuals can appreciate.[2] For example,

---

1. Richard Rohr, from the foreword to *Following Jesus: Finding Our Way Home in an Age of Anxiety*, by Henri J. M. Nouwen, ed. Gabrielle Earnshaw (New York: Convergent, 2019), 10.

2. For more on the spirit of "mentors in ordinariness" see my book *The Tao of Ordinariness* (New York: Oxford University Press, 2019) in which I had the space to focus more deeply on a number of the aspects of understanding and embracing humility and simplicity in a narcissistic age.

renowned author and Holocaust survivor Elie Wiesel described what he considered an ideal experience of mentoring in his relationship with Rebbe Menachem Schneerson, one of the most influential rabbis in modern history. Wiesel said to a Chabad audience, "I know of no one who left the Rebbe without being deeply affected if not changed by the encounter.... Time in his presence begins running at a different pace.... In his presence, you come closer in touch with your inner center of gravity. Whenever I would see the Rebbe, he touched the depths in me. That was true of everyone who came to see the Rebbe. Somehow, when the person left, he or she felt that they had lived deeper and ...on a higher level."[3]

When Schneerson himself was asked by a young boy, "What's a Rebbe good for?" he didn't respond with a feeling of having been insulted or being shown disrespect. Instead he replied, "I can't speak for myself, but I can tell you about my own Rebbe. [He] was the geologist of the soul. You see, there are so many treasures in the earth. There is gold, there is silver, and there are diamonds. But if you don't know where to dig, you'll only find dirt and rocks and mud. The Rebbe can tell you where to dig, and what to dig for, but the digging you must do for yourself."[4]

May we have the good fortune to meet someone like this in our lives. For me, one such person was Henri

---

3. Elie Wiesel, "Greatness," April 7, 1992, available at https://www.chabad.org/therebbe/article_cdo/aid/143509/jewish/Greatness.htm.

4. Joseph Telushkin, *Rebbe: The Life and Teachings of Menachem M. Schneerson, the Most Influential Rabbi in Modern History* (New York: Harper Wave, 2016), 209.

Nouwen. He would ask important questions not only of those who sought his guidance but also of himself. That is one of the main reasons he could mentor others so well — he remained open to those who could teach him something new.

He was willing to share his own fears and darkness, recognizing that they were not reasons to give up. Paradoxically, as we have seen in the comments made by sages such as Nouwen and others, they were transformed over time to be even more present to their ordinary selves and to those who needed their compassion and made them more open to God, just as the *ammas* and *abbas* of the desert once were.

Like all of them, we who set out to care for, or mentor, others will become discouraged at times. We will experience the pain of personal and social injustice. Not to do so would be tantamount to being spiritually dead. We all must face the trap of despair and the temptation to withdraw from the call to be fully alive and deeply compassionate. Mentors like Nouwen model how we must embrace the necessary cross of honest presence to ourselves, to the world, and to God so that we can better know what is true and continue bringing God's light into the world through our compassion.

For years we have heard adages such as, "Children close their ears to advice, but open their eyes to example." What will our example be? If we feel our example must be total perfection and success, we will only run away, or eventually fall away. The odds are too great and we are too frail. Like the suffering professionals in mental health, medicine, ministry, social work, and education, we all need to remember that if we expect perfection of ourselves we will only become deflated rather than re-dedicated each time we fall. Instead, the message of spiritual mentorship is that we are called to be faithful, open, hopeful, self-aware, present, prayerful, and people without guile. And being without guile isn't the same as being without sin; it is an attitude of simplicity and transparency which leads us to become keenly aware of who we are and to acknowledge and embrace our identity — our ordinariness — in order to greet others with grace and humility and stand with them in their darkness without illusion.

During her late adolescent years my daughter, Michaele, once said to me in a burst of candor, "When I was very young everything had to be so 'nice' at the dinner table, and I didn't want to come. Now, I feel when we come together we can be real and say what we feel. We can even disagree! One or both of us may get angry but I know that it is all right. Now I want to come to dinner to be with you and Mom, and this makes me happy."

The honest words of an adolescent, aware of her own feelings and attuned to her parents, cut to the heart of the matter. They show us at a deeper level what we say we already know: "good" family images and the deception marked by "chronic niceness" can often prevent the possibility for real intimacy and growth. They remind us that the darkness outside of ourselves is dangerous only when we are steeped in secrets and continue to hide what we believe to be the darkness within us, our family, our church, our country, or even from God. In my daughter's words (which indicated the good that results when we can be free of playing games and putting on psychological disguises) I could hear echoes of God's words in the Garden of Eden when Adam and Eve were ashamed. God asked, "Who told you that you were naked?" Or, in today's language, "Who told you that you needed to make believe you are something other than who you are? As your God, I know you as you really are and love you. Why don't you believe me?"

Henri Nouwen, in his constant search for unconditional love — and the angst such a search produces — yearned to experience this in certain people, and certainly in God. Yet, alongside this desire remained a hope, optimism, and expressive energy that told us and reminded him: Don't give up hope. It is no surprise then that those who knew him well, such as Michael Higgins, would view him as "a pioneer of the soul."[5]

This book has been about Henri's mentoring spirit shared in person and in letters, as well as through his books, tapes, and lectures. It has also, and to a great extent, been about my own responses to his themes and suggestions. In addition, and most importantly, it has been a call for you to pause, reflect, and note your own ways of embracing the words of mentoring offered to you.

My hope, my goal for you is that you will benefit from Nouwen's presence in order to launch, re-launch, or reorient you on your own journey of living your faith and perhaps mentoring others in the process and so discover your own most complete sense of meaning and self.[6]

My own experiences of mentoring from Henri led me to take the next step by mentoring myself each day. I knew that I would need to put certain aims forward in my life. I knew that they would be simply goals, not realities, given

5. Michael W. Higgins, *Henri Nouwen: A Spirituality for the Wounded*, 5 CDs (Now You Know Media, 2013).

6. For a more complete treatment of mentoring yourself, see my book, *The Simple Care of a Hopeful Heart: Mentoring Yourself in Difficult Times* (New York: Oxford University Press, 2021).

my own limited talents and personal growing edges. For me, these next steps included:

- balancing gentleness with clarity in the questions asked of me—especially those that touch upon areas about which I am unsure, defensive, or sensitive

- providing the mental setting for myself to experiment with new thinking and to find essential truths upon which to base my life more securely

- demonstrating faith in myself even when I fail and resist insight and change

- allowing myself the psychological space to "speak to think" rather than feel everything I recognize has to be thoroughly thought out first

- encouraging myself to be myself by not fearing rejection or ridicule

- helping myself recognize that having a healthy perspective is key in facing and learning from difficult times; in the end, it is not the amount of darkness in the world or us that matters, but how we stand in the darkness with as healthy a perspective as possible

- not asking myself to emulate my role models by "impersonating" them but to have a sense of authenticity and ordinariness that gives me the courage to be me

- being open to a broad approach to searching further when I am lost, so that I don't seek someone else's answers but strive to find my own

- having the sensitivity to appreciate my own sense of "lostness" when what I thought I knew no longer suffices

We will know if we are taking steps such as these in the best way possible because we will also:

- begin to sound and behave more in accordance with beliefs we have examined rather than with what the world is saying is valuable or true

- seek to find, more fully understand, enjoy, and share all of our signature strengths — not only the obvious ones

- catch ourselves when we only emphasize the negative feedback we give ourselves and play down the gifts we have been given that others are grateful for

- be able to listen to criticism but be discerning in how we are going to embrace and grow from it

- know that mentoring ourselves is a never-ending pilgrimage toward living life to the fullest, and that we have to continue on the journey with meaning, compassion, and joy in this world

To be sure, though, embracing such themes and values as desert wisdom, ordinariness, compassion, and vulnerability and prayer, come at a cost. They may not play well with some of the ways we are now viewing ourselves and the world—especially during times of stress, family need, trauma, pandemic, divisions in our communities, in our country or the church, or even simply personal discomfort. However, if we don't look away, darkness can also promise and deliver something we are all looking for in life. It requires viewing dark times with a deep sense of being loved by God, a love that is reflected in the beauty of nature, simple encounters with people and animals that provide us with joy, and those quiet refreshing spiritual moments when we are alone.

Once again, in the words of Henri Nouwen:

Maybe it is exactly the experience of loneliness that allows us to describe the first tentative lines of solitude. Maybe it is precisely the shocking confrontation with our hostile self that gives us words to speak about hospitality as a real option, and maybe we will never find the courage to speak about prayer as a human vocation without the disturbing discovery of our own illusions. Often it is the dark forest that makes us speak about the open field. Frequently prison makes us think about freedom, hunger helps us to appreciate food, and war gives us words for peace. Not seldom are our visions of the future born out of the sufferings of the present and our hope for others out of our own despair. Only few "happy endings" make us happy, but often someone's careful and honest articulations of the ambiguities, uncertainties and painful conditions of life give us new hope. The paradox is indeed that new life is born out of the pains of the old.[7]

The recent spirituality of suffering literature and post-traumatic growth (PTG)[8] echoes the hope contained in the paradox Nouwen mentions. Especially in the case of post-traumatic growth, we are told that when we don't play down the darkness we experience (which would simply be an exercise in "spiritual romanticism"), and when we remain open to where it might take us, something unusual and beautiful may happen. We may experience new depth, a deeper appreciation of life, and a new sense of meaning-making that would not have been possible had the trauma or darkness not have happened in the first place. The life and work of Nouwen bears this out as he calls all of us to honesty, commitment, and hope, even in the darkest moments of life.

In it is the very darkness of life, in a world where the so-called proofs of personal worth—namely, success, fame, attractiveness, and influence—are touted as necessary requirements for achieving happiness, Henri Nouwen shows us what they really are: empty. Then he reveals where true happiness is to be found. By demonstrating his almost childlike enthusiasm for God while simultaneously sharing his own restlessness, psychological wounds, and spiritual frailties, he reminds us that he is a loved child of God—even amidst pain and doubts—and that we are too!

---

7. Henri J. M. Nouwen, *Reaching Out: The Three Movements of the Spiritual Life* (New York: Image Books, 1986), 11.

8. For more on posttraumatic growth, see my books *Perspective: The Calm within the Storm* and *The Simple Care of a Hopeful Heart* both published by Oxford University Press.

Sources Cited

Works by Henri J. M. Nouwen

Beyond the Mirror: Reflections on Life and Death. New York: Crossroad, 2001.

Clowning in Rome: Reflections on Solitude, Celibacy, Prayer, and Contemplation. New York: Image Books, 2000.

(with Donald McNeill and Douglas Morrison) *Compassion: A Reflection on the Christian Life.* New York: Image Books, 2006.

The Genesee Diary: Report from a Trappist Monastery. New York: Image Books, 1981.

The Inner Voice of Love: A Journey through Anguish to Freedom. New York: Image Books, 1999.

Letters to Marc about Jesus: Living a Spiritual Life in a Material World. New York: HarperOne, 2009.

Life of the Beloved: Spiritual Living in a Secular World. New York: Crossroad, 2002.

The Living Reminder: Service and Prayer in Memory of Jesus Christ. New York: HarperOne, 2009.

Making All Things New: An Invitation to the Spiritual Life. New York: HarperCollins, 1981.

Out of Solitude: Three Meditations on the Christian Life. Notre Dame, IN: Ave Maria Press, 2004.

Reaching Out: The Three Movements of the Spiritual Life. New York: Image Books, 1986.

The Return of the Prodigal Son: A Story of Homecoming. New York: Image Books, 1994).

The Way of the Heart: Connecting with God through Prayer, Wisdom, and Silence. New York: Ballantine, 2003.

Works by Other Authors

Bloom, Anthony. *Beginning to Pray Beginning to Pray.* New York: Paulist Press, 1970.

Buber, Martin. *Tales of the Hasidim Tales of the Hasidim.* New York: Schocken Books, 1991.

Burton-Christie, Douglas. *The Word in the Desert: Scripture and the Quest for Holiness in Early Christian Monasticism.* New York: Oxford University Press.

Gallagher, Fr. Joseph. "Fr. Henri Nouwen of Happy Memory." *National Catholic Reporter,* November 15, 1996.

Gibran, Kahlil. *Sand and Foam.* New York: Knopf, 1966.

Heschel, Abraham Joshua. *I Asked for Wonder: A Spiritual Anthology.* New York: Crossroad, 1986.

Housden, Roger. *Ten Poems to Change Your Life.* New York: Harmony Books, 2001.

Krishnamurti, Jiddu. *Life Ahead: On Learning and the Search for Meaning.* Novato, CA: New World Library, 2005.

Langewiesche, William. *Sahara Unveiled: A Journey across the Desert*. New York: Vintage, 1997.

Lawrence of the Resurrection, Brother. *The Practice of the Presence of God*. Translated by John J. Delaney. New York: Image Books, 1977.

McFague, Sallie. *Models of God*. Philadelphia: Fortress Press, 1987.

Merton, Thomas. *The Wisdom of the Desert: Sayings from the Desert Fathers of the Fourth Century*. Boston: Shambhala, 2004.

Nelson, Gertrud Mueller. *Here All Dwell Free: Stories to Heal the Wounded Feminine*. New York: Paulist Press, 1999.

Nomura, Yushi. *Desert Wisdom: Sayings from the Desert Fathers*. Maryknoll, NY: Orbis Books, 2001.

Rilke, Rianer Maria. *Letters to a Young Poet*. New York: Norton, 1934.

Telushkin, Joseph. *Rebbe: The Life and Teachings of Menachem M. Schneerson, the Most Influential Rabbi in Modern History*. New York: Harper Wave, 2016.

Ward, Benedicta. *The Sayings of the Desert Fathers: The Alphabetical Collection*. Collegeville, MN: Cistercian Publications, 1984.

Wicks, Robert J. *The Simple Care of a Hopeful Heart: Mentoring Yourself in Difficult Times*. New York: Oxford University Press, 2021.

———. *The Tao of Ordinariness: Humility and Simplicity in a Narcissistic Age*. New York: Oxford University Press, 201).

For Further Reading

There are a number of wonderful biographies of Henri Nouwen as well as serious reflections on his life and ministry. As in the case of the ones of Thomas Merton, each provides a unique vantage point of a complex human being. Ones that I would especially recommend include:

Beumer, Jurjen. *Henri Nouwen: A Restless Seeking for God*. New York: Crossroad, 1998.

Burns, Kevin. *Henri Nouwen: His Life and Spirit*. Cincinnati: Franciscan Media, 2016.

De Vinck, Christopher. *Nouwen Then: Personal Reflections on Henri*. Grand Rapids, MI: Zondervan, 1999.

Ford, Michael. *Wounded Prophet: A Portrait of Henri J. M. Nouwen*. New York: Crown, 2002.

Hernandez, Wil. *Henri Nouwen and Soul Care: A Ministry of Integration*. New York: Paulist Press, 2008.

———. *Henri Nouwen: A Spirituality of Imperfection*. New York: Paulist Press, 2006.

Higgins, Michael, and Kevin Burns. *Genius Born of Anguish: The Life and Legacy of Henri Nouwen*. New York: Paulist Press, 2012.

LaNoue, Deirdre. *The Spiritual Legacy of Henri Nouwen.* New York: Continuum, 2000.

O'Laughlin, Michael. *God's Beloved: A Spiritual Biography of Henri Nouwen.* Maryknoll, NY: Orbis Books, 2004.

———. *Henri Nouwen: His Life and Vision.* Maryknoll, NY: Orbis Books, 2009.

Porter, Beth (ed.) with Susan M. S. Brown and Philip Coulter. *Befriending Life: Encounters with Henri Nouwen.* New York: Image Books, 2002.

Twomey, Gerald S., and Claude Pomerleau (eds.). *Remembering Henri: The Life and Legacy of Henri Nouwen.* Maryknoll, NY: Orbis Books, 2006.

There are also numerous collections of selections from his writings and letters. These include:

Durback, Robert (ed.). *Seeds of Hope: A Henri Nouwen Reader.* New York: Image Books, 1997.

Earnshaw, Gabrielle (ed.). *Love, Henri: Letters on the Spiritual Life.* New York: Convergent Books, 2018.

Ford, Michael (ed.). *A Restless Soul: Meditations from the Road.* Notre Dame, IN: Ave Maria Press, 2008.

———. *Behold the Beauty of the Lord: Praying with Icons.* Notre Dame, IN: Ave Maria Press, 2007.

———. *Eternal Seasons: A Spiritual Journey through the Church's Year.* Notre Dame, IN: Ave Maria Press, 2007.

Greer, Wendy Wilson (ed.). *The Only Necessary Thing – Living a Prayerful Life*. New York: Crossroad, 2008.

Jonas, Robert A. (ed.). *Henri Nouwen: Selections*. Maryknoll, NY: Orbis Books, 1998.

Laird, Rebecca, and Michael J. Christensen (eds.). *The Heart of Henri Nouwen: His Words of Blessing*. New York: Crossroad, 2003.

Nouwen, Henri. *Jesus: A Gospel*, ed. by Michael O'Laughlin. Maryknoll, NY: Orbis Books, 2013.

————. *Spiritual Direction: Wisdom for the Long Walk of Faith*. New York: HarperOne, 2015.

————. *Spiritual Formation: Following the Movements of the Spirit*. New York: HarperOne, 2015.

Nouwen, Henri, with Michael J. Christensen and Rebecca Laird. *Discernment: Reading the Signs of Daily Life*. New York: HarperOne, 2015.

Finally, I recommend the twelve lectures on five CDs by Michael Higgins, entitled *Henri Nouwen: A Spirituality for the Wounded* from Now You Know Media/Learn25 Productions, and the DVD *Journey of the Heart: The Life of Henri Nouwen* presented by Windborne Productions in Canada.

In the biographies listed above you will find a complete listing of Henri Nouwen's writings as well.

Acknowledgments and Permissions

I didn't quite realize how much I loved writing until a college friend of mine, whom I hadn't seen for quite a while, asked me when we finally got together again, "How many books have you published?" When I told him, he paused for a moment, blinked, smiled, and said, "Bob, I really think you need to get out more often!" and we both laughed.

And so, for me to write another book now, I felt there had to be a need to experience something anew, afresh, otherwise there would be serious doubts as to whether it made real sense to undertake the project. In the case of *Let's Look Together*, the compelling nature of addressing four of the beautiful mentoring themes of Henri Nouwen was clear. I wanted to once again, more intentionally, sit quietly and reflect—this time, possibly more deeply—on some of the key spiritual messages this true spiritual mentor made available. In doing this, I also wanted to consider the ways I have sought to take them further. My hope was that this might then open up the door for *you* to do so as well—with both Henri's ideas and some of mine.

And so, while I know that the idea for this book was sparked by the wisdom of Henri Nouwen, I also recognize that what and how I have selected from his writings, letters to me, and comments made in our two meetings, says something about me as well. In these pages, I know I have also indicated a great deal about my own interests, values, challenges, and spirituality. I have consciously sought to take to heart what Nouwen's beliefs were and build on them, make them my own... *and take them a step further.*

What you find particularly helpful for you will also say a great deal about *you* and where you are in the spiritual life at this point. It is with this understanding, and the belief that what you have read is written to call you to do the same as I have—given your own life and calling at this point—that I share this with you.

I am pleased that Oxford University Press has given me permission to adapt some material from *The Tao of Ordinariness: Humility and Simplicity in a Narcissistic Age* and *The Simple Care of a Hopeful Heart: Mentoring Yourself in Difficult Times* since the psychological material in them is so much in line with what I have written about spirituality in *Let's Look Together.* I also wish to thank Ave Maria Press for originally publishing both *Seeds of Sensitivity* and *Crossing the Desert* which are now out of print. I feel they represented some of my best early writing and, upon close inspection, contained some necessary material and information well-suited to adapt and update for this new work. Excerpts from *The Genesee Diary: Report from a Trappist Monastery* by Henri Nouwen, copyright © 1976 by Henri J. M. Nouwen, copyright renewed © 2004 by Sue Mosteller, CSJ, executrix of the Estate of Henri J. M. Nouwen, are used by permission of Doubleday, an imprint of the Knopf Doubleday Publishing Group, a division of Penguin Random House LLC. All rights reserved.

I would also like to express my gratitude to Jon Sweeney who has served as my editor in two publishing houses. His wisdom is always a help... but I like his enthusiasm even better! Finally, as always, I would like to thank my wife Michaele for her editorial suggestions. My books are always better when I have taken them.

About the Author

For more than forty years, Dr. Robert Wicks has been called upon by individuals and groups experiencing great stress, anxiety, and confusion to speak calm into chaos. Wicks received his doctorate in psychology (Psy.D.) from Hahnemann Medical College and Hospital, is professor emeritus at Loyola University Maryland, and has taught in universities and professional schools of psychology, medicine, nursing, theology, education, and social work. In 2003 he was the commencement speaker for Wright State School of Medicine in Dayton, Ohio, and in 2005 he was visiting scholar and commencement speaker at Stritch School of Medicine in Chicago. He was also the recipient of honorary doctorates from Georgian Court, Caldwell, and Marywood universities.

Over the past several years he has spoken on his major areas of expertise—resilience, self-care, and the prevention of secondary stress (pressures encountered in reaching out to others)—on Capitol Hill to members of Congress and their chiefs of staff, at Johns Hopkins School of Medicine, the U.S. Air Force Academy, the Mayo Clinic, the North American Aerospace Defense Command, the U.S. Army Medical Command, and the Defense Intelligence Agency, as well as at Boston's Children's Hospital, Harvard Divinity School, Yale School of Nursing, Princeton Theological Seminary, and to members of the NATO Intelligence Fusion Center in England. He spoke at the Boston Public Library's commemoration of the Boston Marathon bombing, addressed ten thousand educators in the Air Canada Arena in Toronto, has given presentations at the FBI and New York City Police Academies, was the opening keynote speaker to fifteen hundred physicians for the American Medical Directors Association, led a course on resilience in Beirut for relief workers from Aleppo, Syria, and addressed caregivers in twenty different countries, including China, Vietnam, India, Thailand, Haiti, Northern Ireland, Hungary, Guatemala, Malta, New Zealand, Australia, France, England, and South Africa.

In 1994, he was responsible for the psychological debriefing of NGO staffers/relief workers evacuated from Rwanda during the genocide there. In 1993, and again in 2001, he worked in Cambodia with professionals from the English-speaking community who were present to help the Khmer people rebuild their nation following years of terror and torture. In 2006, he delivered presentations on self-care at the National Naval Medical Center in Bethesda Maryland and Walter Reed Army Hospital to those health care professionals responsible for Iraq and Afghan war veterans. More recently, he addressed U.S. Army health care professionals returning from Africa where they were assisting during the Ebola crisis.

Dr. Wicks has published over sixty books for both professionals and the general public, including the bestselling *Riding the Dragon*. Among his latest books are *The Simple Care of a Hopeful Heart; Perspective: The Calm within the Storm*, and *Bounce: Living the Resilient Life*. His books for professionals include *Overcoming Secondary Stress in Medical and Nursing Practice* (second edition with Gloria Donnelly), and *The Resilient Clinician.* In 2006, Dr. Wicks received the alumni award for excellence in professional psychology from Widener University. He is also the recipient of the humanitarian of the year award from the American Counseling Association's Division on Spirituality, Ethics and Religious Values in Counseling. For his service to the Roman Catholic Church, he is the recipient of the papal medal, *Pro Ecclesia et Pontifice.* He lives in West Chester, Pennsylvania.